My Bundle of Early Life

Linda Gholston

Copyright © 2018 by Linda Gholston
Illustrator and Cover Design Brenda Ragsdale
Illustrator Brenda "Sam" Mols

All rights reserved. No part of this publication may be reproduced, distributed, or transmitted in any form or by any means, including photocopying, recording, or other electronic or mechanical methods, without the prior written permission of the publisher, except in the case of brief quotations embodied in critical reviews and certain other noncommercial uses permitted by copyright law.

Scripture quotations marked (NLT) are taken from the Holy Bible, New Living Translation, copyright ©1996, 2004, 2015 by Tyndale House Foundation. Used by permission of Tyndale House Publishers, Inc., Carol Stream, Illinois 60188. All rights reserved.

Scriptures marked KJV are taken from the KING JAMES VERSION (KJV): KING JAMES VERSION, public domain.

ISBN: 978-1-7907971-6-5

Liberation's Publishing LLC
West Point, Mississippi
www.liberationspublishing.com

Dedication

To those who call me GAL

*"...with my eyes I traced the line
of the horizon thin and fine
Straight around till I was come
Back to where I'd started."*

*Edna St. Vicent Milley
(1892-1950)*

Contents

Introduction 9

Preface 11

Baby's Shoes... Momma's Blues 15

A September Christmas 19

Deflation 25

Magic Egg 29

What's in the Well 37

Hobos and Pies 43

Mourning and Forgiving 47

Looking Back 51

Sowing and Reaping 55

Salvation 61

Scotty Kim 65

Revival and Dry Cleaning 71

My Sister and Me 75

My Brother Charlie 81

Answered Prayer 91

Spiritual Note 95

The Chiropractor 97

Healing 101

Sitting Up with The Sick 107

Daddy's Down 111

Ducks on a Pond 117

Ma's Company 121

Mrs. Gordon and Nancy 129

Measuring Head Circumference 133

Earliest Remembrance 141

Teamwork 145

Aunt Tannis 149

Sayings 157

Sign Language 161

Dan For Christmas 167

Christmas Day 175

Uncle Bulich 177

Stay with Me 183

How Many Cows 189

Winter of '56 197

Whiskey 201

Mama's Prize 205

Women of Substance 207

Purse on the Bridge 213

Hog Killing Day 217

Goats 227

Wisdom 233

Values 239

House on Fire 247

Buster 253

Lois and Billy Graham 261

Daddy and the Greased Pig 269

Honey Bee in Diaper Shirt 273

Young Joe B 277

Broken Crayons Still Color 283

Little Goody Two Shoes 287

In appreciation... 295

To Those Who Call Me 'GAL' 297

Linda Gholston

Introduction

For several years I have felt the urge to write a book. Not a book for the masses but for a few who enjoy short snippets about farm life in the 50's and 60's, as viewed through the eyes of one born in 1947. This is not intended to be a historical document. I may have some dates wrong, but they are as close as I can get them. I may not recall the people as they truly were but as I saw them through my young naïve lenses. **They are who they were to me**.

These stories are not intended to be fictional writing. All or most happened as recorded according to my recollection. The names are real, except in a couple of cases where I thought it best to change names so no current descendants would be recognized or offended in anyway.

This book is not intended to be a scholarly journal. God has blessed me with some vivid recalls of my younger years. I have written these vignettes without a lot of thought to sentence structure. The stories are written in the vernacular we used during the time I was growing up. I pray I did an acceptable job with spelling and did not dangle too many participles, but a grade wasn't in my thinking as I wrote.

The intent of *"A Bundle of Early Life"* is simply to record for my family and others who are interested, remembrances of growing up in Pratt. Nothing more; nothing less.

This afternoon as I write, I'm sitting on the front porch of my house (built in 2005). I am looking at the hay field, the corn patch, the pasture with a few horses. To my left is Mama's and Daddy's house (built in 1953). This is where Keylon and I grew up. Straight ahead is Ma and Pa Gholston's house (built in 1890's). To my right is Keylon & Teresa's house (built in 1981). Much of the scene is the same as the time from which I write, and much is different. Such is life.

Some aspects of Gholston Farm have varied, but the joy of life here remains constant. No matter where I have lived, worked or traveled, the longing for the farm has always been.

In these memories I have the blessing of returning to the time, place and people who molded me, taught me, inspired me and "grew" me. **Come with me...**

Preface

David was grieving, angry, hungry and constantly on guard for his life. Even though he was chosen as Israel's next King, David was running for his life from Israel's current King, Saul.

He had hidden in caves and forests and had resisted the opportunity to kill Saul. David had just attended the burial of Samuel in Ramah, and along with about six hundred warriors had fled to the wilderness of Paran.

It so happened that it was sheep shearing time. A very harsh and evil man, Nabal, had his sheep there being sheered. David and his men protected the sheep shearers, the sheep and the bundles of wool.

Soon, David and his men became hungry so on a feast day he sent ten of his men to humbly ask Nabal to share nourishment with them.

Nabal refused the request and actually scoffed at David. His ten men returned and reported Nabal's reply to David. Rage filled every fiber of David's being.

Immediately, David announced that at the light of day, he and four hundred men would ride and kill Nabal and all males in his company. This would include any sons, servants and animals. In David's mind it would be a day of slaughter and bloodshed.

A smart young man who was employed by Nabal overheard the exchange and knew that danger loomed. He reported the incident to Nabal's wife, the beautiful and intelligent Abigail.

With no hesitation, she instructed servants to load several donkeys with all kinds of food. Then, bravely Abigail set out to meet David.

As four hundred and one horses pounded the path, small Abigail stood in a pass between the mountains. David had only two choices. He could simply plow her down and leave a greasy spot or he could stop. He chose the latter.

As Abigail spoke, she showed great humility and actually accepted responsibility for this action in which she played no part. Her interest at this point was not her horrible husband but her future King. She implored David to not have this blood on his hands.

Then she says the most remarkable comment:

Yet a man is risen to pursue thee, and to seek thy soul: but the soul of my lord shall be bound in the bundle of life with the LORD thy God; and the souls of thine enemies, them shall he sling out, as out of the middle of a sling. (KJV)

In the New Living Translation, she says, "God's treasure pouch".

To me, this is one of the most endearing promises we as Christians have. We are held in "God's bundle of life" or "God's treasure pouch."

Ten years of serving at Sanctuary Hospice House taught me that all of us have our own "bundles of life." This book is simply a compilation of events that are important, special, and meaningful from my childhood.

So, when it came time to choose a title for these remembrances I knew immediately that I would call it "My Bundle of Early Life."

Linda Gholston

Baby's Shoes... Momma's Blues

In August 1957, Keylon was ten months old and Mama wanted to have a professional photographer take pictures of him. She read in the newspaper that Olan Mills™ would be in Tupelo for three days. The advertisement featured babies. Some were sitting in wash tubs, some on blankets, others posed in front of a beach scene. Several times Mama and Daddy discussed the possibility of having the pictures made. The main issue was money. Could we afford it? Finally, they decided if we ordered the least expensive package we could do it. Mama began to make the preparations.

She had been to The Corner Shoe Store in Tupelo about a month before and bought Keylon's first pair of Buster Brown shoes. In the 50's it was believed that babies must have sturdy, hard sole shoes as they began to walk. Also, she bought him a yellow diaper shirt with matching bloomers that fit over his diaper. After much discussion it was decided this was what the baby would wear for his "first ever" picture.

We didn't have a telephone, but Pa and Ma Gholston did. Mama used their phone to call and make the appointment. We were to be there at two o'clock on Wednesday. Excitement galore!

Aunt B drove us to Tupelo in her 1954 Ford. She, Mama, and the baby were on the front seat while I sat in the back. Seat belts were a thing of the future, so I had lots of room to move about and feel the hot air that blew in from all four windows being rolled down. It was very hot!

Mama knew we would arrive with our hair all windblown, so she took the Johnson's baby oil and hair brush. Keylon would look his best in the pictures.

We arrived. The photographer had a thick black cloth spread over a table and sat Keylon in the center as he said to Mama, "this is the cutest baby I've seen all day". We beamed with pride. It never dawned on me that he said this about all the babies.

As a ten-month-old child Keylon sat like a little man with his legs straight out toward the camera. Mama fixed his socks and wiped a little drool off his chin. The man began to take pictures with bright bulbs flashing. Keylon liked the lights, and he smiled and laughed perfectly. Mama was delighted!

She paid and signed the forms, being careful to order the least expensive package. The photographer explained that we would receive the packet in six to eight weeks including one eight by ten, two five by sevens and eight wallet sized prints. (We called "wallets" "billfolds".) On the way home, Mama and B discussed who would receive these prizes! I could only imagine how much everyone would love getting one of these pictures. Of course, the eight by ten would go on our fireboard! (The mantle was called a "fireboard".)

As time neared for the package to arrive, Mama would eagerly watch for the mailman. As soon as she saw his truck pull up and deposit mail we would head to the box before his truck was out of sight. One day Mama reached in and got the mail and exclaimed, "Here they are!" As I held Keylon tightly, I knew that the large, brown manila envelope contained the prized pictures.

Mama opened it right there in the dirt road where we stood. She looked like a kid at Christmas! Carefully, she slid the cardboard protector out and pulled the eight by ten close to her face. Instantly she began to cry and quietly said, "Linda Joy, you have ruined these pictures!" Me? What had I done? I didn't know whether to run or stay. My curiosity got the best of me, and I peeked in the envelope to see what had so upset Mama.

There it was. Keylon's shoes being nearest to the camera appeared larger than they actually were. The bottoms of those Buster Brown shoes had a message I had written soon after they were bought. In my nine-year-old mind I thought everyone loved and wanted that baby as much as I did, so I wanted a way for him to be quickly identified should someone kidnap him. So, on his right shoe, plain as day, I had written, "My name is Keylon

Gholston" and on the left shoe was written, "This is my picture" and, I drew him as best I could.

Mama cried for three days, Daddy just shook his head. I thought I saw the slightest grin on his face, but I knew not to tell Mama. I also knew Daddy understood my heart.

A September Christmas

Ma Gholston seldom went into town. She did most of her shopping with peddlers. They drove rolling stores – enclosed trucks with shelving. From the peddlers, Ma Gholston could purchase staple goods such as flour, meal, sugar, canned goods, cleaning supplies, and occasionally, candy!

Ma's favorite peddler was Peddler Payne. He was an older gentleman with white hair who was very courteous and kind. He would get out of the truck and put a wooden step down to the ground so that Ma could walk up into the truck.

Also, once a month the Watkins man would call on Ma and Pa Gholston. This was Brother Gassaway, and over the years they became very good friends. It was not unusual for him to sit by the fireplace and visit all afternoon on a cold blustery winter day. He was quite a Bible scholar, and we all enjoyed listening to his soothing, confident voice. A learned man.

He traveled in a black Studebaker car. There was a large wooden case in the "turtle shell" with many compartments. (The "turtle shell" would later be referred to as the trunk of a vehicle). He had a smaller wooden carrier in which he would put the items he thought Ma and Pa might need, and he would bring it into the house. Always, he had vanilla and lemon flavoring, black pepper and liniment plus a variety of tonics and salves. Occasionally Ma and Pa would buy a bottle of turpentine as both used it to prevent various illnesses.

Every night my Pa Gholston would sit on the side of his bed and pick up the turpentine bottle which he kept on a small wooden stool. He would firmly press the opening of the bottle on the top of his tongue and turn it up. Very quickly he would lower it. So, just the tiny amount that touched his tongue was his "dose", after which he would swallow a couple of times, lie down and pull the covers over his bald head. This was performed almost like a ritual. Obviously, the room reeked of turpentine.

My favorite peddler was a man small in stature but large in heart. His name was Brownie. Ma Gholston preferred Peddler Payne because one day she had smelled alcohol when Brownie spoke. Being a teetotaler and not believing in the consumption of any alcoholic beverages, she had feared that Brownie might buy liquor with cash, so she mainly "bartered" with him. She would have several dozen extra eggs most weeks and he loved getting the fresh farm eggs to sell to others.

Although Peddler Payne got the bulk of her business Ma Gholston always swapped eggs for merchandise she needed with Brownie. On most every visit he would give me a piece of bubble gum and we would chat for as long as he could stay. Somehow, as

I watched Brownie's truck go out the long driveway I always felt special and important! It appeared all I had was a piece of gum but in fact I had a lot more. Brownie, through simple gestures of conversation and interest, gave me a sense of "specialness". At an early age, from the peddler, I learned one of the most valuable lessons of my life.

One hot summer day Brownie asked me what I wanted for Christmas. I really hadn't thought about Christmas, but I knew what my heart longed for – wheels, a little bicycle I could ride. Daddy and Uncle Bulich had tractor wheels, Aunt B had a car and an old 26-inch bicycle, but my feet wouldn't touch the peddles. I wanted a little bike like my neighbor, Larry, had. So, not being a shy child, I explained to Brownie exactly what I wanted. Then reality hit, and I was reminded that Christmas was an eternity away. Little did I realize what a smart, creative salesman Brownie was or that our conversation would ever cross his mind again.

In September, Mama, Daddy, and Uncle Bulich were harvesting crops. Pa was busy in his orchard and Aunt B was teaching school. Ma Gholston and I were at the house where she was cooking three meals a day for the farmhands. I spent a lot of time with her; occasionally, I would go outside and ride my stick horse that was an old mop handle. My Uncle Bulich had carefully bored a small hole through the handle and attached a rope. I don't recall ever naming the horse because after all it was a mop handle with a rope attached. But once I got on my "horse" I rode fearlessly, killing bandits and outlaws.

This is just what I was doing one afternoon when I looked up and saw Brownie's blue peddling truck slow down and begin to turn into our place. I ran into the house to tell Ma the peddler was coming. An overjoyed child, I would have someone to talk to for a while and new gum for my Bayer Aspirin tin which housed "my chew" from day to day. This is a trick I learned from Pa Gholston!

As I got back outside Brownie was backing in under the big oak tree and getting the ladder out and ready for Ma. Suddenly, I saw him roll a little blue bicycle down that handmade ladder. My heart stopped! "Where's your daddy?" Brownie asked.

"In 'the bottom' pulling corn," I said, almost whispering. Guess I was afraid I'd wake from a dream.

"Run and get him. I've brought you a bicycle."

I ran to the corn patch as fast as my fat short legs would go. (Wish I had thought to borrow the bike.) Finally, I saw Daddy on his gray Ferguson tractor. I waved my arms and shouted at him until I got his attention. He stopped the tractor and asked me "What's the matter"?

"Nothing," I shouted over the tractor's engine, "Brownie wants to see you. He has a bicycle for me."

"Oh, my goodness", Daddy mumbled, "I don't have time for this." As he grumbled he was picking me up, sitting me on his lap and off we went for the house.

We got there and there stood Brownie with the little used blue bicycle – love at second sight for me. He and Daddy talked. Brownie wanted seventy-five cents, but Daddy said it wasn't worth more than fifty cents and that was his best offer.

I got really scared. They haggled, each spitting chewing tobacco as they laughed and talked. The bicycle didn't seem nearly as important to them as it was to me.

Finally, Daddy said he had to get back to the field. His phrase was, "I'm burning day light." He said good bye to Brownie and headed toward his tractor. Brownie headed toward his peddling truck.

My heart sank. There went my bike. So close, yet so far. I could see me on the mop handle for years to come. Sad...

Suddenly, Brownie turned around and hollered out, "Ok, Douglas. I bought this with your girl in mind. Give me fifty cents and we'll call it even."

Wow! I stood perfectly still. I didn't know for sure what "we'll call it even," meant. Daddy paid him two quarters, got on his tractor, and said to me, "Merry Christmas"!

Brownie rolled the bicycle over and presented it with great flare! In that instant I knew that the presenter was as overjoyed as the receiver. Brownie and I had a special bond because he not only made my first bike possible, but he taught me another valuable lesson about joy and delight.

Deflation

When I was six years old I got a basketball from Santa! This had been my request for several months as we attended all the Baldwyn High School basketball games. Mama and Daddy were avid basketball fans, and we seldom missed a game if Daddy could scrap together enough money for tickets and borrow Uncle Bulich's pick-up truck. Sometimes we would ride with Curtis, Lois and Shirley Glenn. Can you imagine six of us in a "one seat" pick-up truck! It wasn't that far, and we didn't care, as long as we were going to a game!

At every game I would lament about how I would love to have a basketball. So, as Christmas approached, it made perfect sense that this would be my request. Now, this was at a time when most kids usually got one gift and maybe some candy, fruit and nuts in one of their daddy's old socks that would be hung on the mantle (fire board).

Of course, I was thrilled on Christmas morning to find a basketball underneath the tree! After breakfast it was time to go to Ma and Pa Gholston's house for Christmas dinner. Such fun! It would be chicken and dressing, vegetables, fruit salad, and special desserts. Also, my cousins from Starkville would be there. Uncle Edd and Aunt Lorene brought Robert Edd and Patricia and all their gifts; we had so much fun playing in the "east room" at Ma Gholston's!

About three o'clock, Uncle Edd announced that they had to leave to visit their other grandparents in the Blackland Community. Aunt Lorene's parents along with her sister, Margaret, would be awaiting their arrival and have more gifts around their tree.

We stood on the front porch and waved until the car was out of sight. The adults then returned to what we called the front room. The room contained two beds, one for Ma and one for Pa plus a couch, and several chairs that were crowded around the hearth of a large, open fireplace.

I wandered out to the back porch with my new basketball. What a treasure! It smelled like leather and felt exactly like I dreamed it would. With plenty of solid flooring, I was a six-year-old, alone with a bouncing ball and my imagination… a train wreck waiting to happen!

As I bounced the ball it occurred to me that something inside was causing it to go up and down. I kept thinking, "What could it be?" As my imagination got into gear I could see all kinds of neat little creatures that just must be inside the basketball causing the motion. Then the thought struck me! What if I had what was inside of the basketball? Wouldn't it be a lot more fun? I could hold the "whatever" it was and have great fun seeing it go up and down! Wow!

So, I went into the house. I didn't go to the front room to ask Mama or Daddy what made the ball go up and down. I thought how wonderful it would be to surprise them with the mysterious entity encased in the ball! Could there be a magical imp inside that caused my ball to bounce up and down?

I slipped into the kitchen and got Ma Gholston's largest knife. Then I wedged the basketball between two concrete blocks and stabbed as if I were killing a tiger. Immediately, air gushed into my face and quickly I made the cut large enough to get my hand into the cavity of the basketball. Lo and behold, nothing was there. My basketball was ruined, and I had no little "magical imp". I went into the front room with my limp basketball and tears streaming down my face. Mama and Daddy seemed to know exactly what had happened.

My Christmas cheer deflated as the air flooded from that basketball.

Magic Egg

For his twelfth birthday my cousin, Robert Edd, got a chemistry set. It was a white, shiny metal case with red writing and chemical symbols. The tin box held an array of powders, liquids, instruments, and equipment. Also, there was a booklet filled with instructions for many experiments.

One experiment that caught our attention was entitled, "How to Make a Magic Egg". The first instruction was a list of items needed: a brown egg, a china cup and ingredients from the kit. Ma had plenty of cups and we disregarded the "china" adjective. The brown egg was no concern as Ma had a pen full of chickens and a refrigerator tray full of eggs. A few were white, but most were a rich, medium brown.

Next, we were to write the message of our choosing with a small paraffin (wax) pencil included in the chemistry set. It was shaped like a crayon but smaller. Robert and I talked at length about the message that would be inscribed on our magic egg. Being the tricksters we were, we decided what fun it would be to play a trick on our neighbor, Mrs. Ozell.

She too had chickens and late every afternoon we would see Mrs. Ozell go into the hallway of the barn to gather eggs. Her husband, Mochie, had hung orange crates made from light, thin wood on the walls. They had filled the crates with hay and this is where her hens laid their eggs each day.

So, we contrived our plan – we would first ask Ma Gholston for an egg. She was the most caring, loving person Robert Edd and I had ever known. Neither of us had any idea that our request for an egg would be denied. We just had to be very careful how we asked. Never would we lie to Ma Gholston. We just might not share the full intent of why we needed the egg. When we told her it was for a chemistry experiment she smiled broadly and said, "Of course y'all can have an egg. Go to the Frigidaire and get the one you want." (This was the brand of her refrigerator, but she always called it 'the Frigidaire'.)

With egg in hand we followed the instructions exactly. First, we were to write our "secret message" on the egg using the small paraffin pencil enclosed in the chemistry set. Next, we were to put one half cup of water into the china cup (we used Pa Gholston's coffee cup). Then, add the ingredient, which was nothing but bleach. Thirdly, we were to drop the egg into the cup and leave it, undisturbed, for at least four hours. The concoction would work its magic!

On a hot July day at 3:05pm (according to the kitchen clock) our egg went into the bleach and water. It seemed to take an eternity but finally, after supper and the dishes were washed, the old clock said three minutes past seven. Close enough!

All adults were on the big front porch listening to The Grand Ole Opry. Pa sat under the dim light where he had one additional electrical plug. He would sit there and hold the radio on his lap and everyone else would sit in swings, chairs, or the steps to listen to their favorites. Among their best liked were Roy Acuff, Buck Owens, Bill Anderson and String Bean. Ma Gholston didn't care for Hank Williams. She said all his music was about whiskey, women, and honky tonks.

Robert Edd took a spoon and fished the egg from the cup. It was white! Except for the "secret message" which was brown just like the entire egg had been at three o'clock.

Now, the final instruction was to gently scrape any of the paraffin used to write the message. We tenderly removed all the residue of paraffin, and had, in our hands, a beautiful white egg with a permanent message written in brown.

Sunday was July $2^{nd,}$ but we would be celebrating the fourth of July as all the men needed to be in the fields on Tuesday. We would enjoy a feast that included a big bucket of lemonade, watermelon from Pa's patch, and homemade ice-cream! Early in the morning Uncle Bulich went to the ice house and bought a fifty-pound block of ice. He wrapped it in one of Ma's old quilts and put it in the back of his pick-up truck. We would use it for ice tea, lemonade, and homemade ice-cream.

No Gholston would be in church that Sunday, but Mrs. Ozell and her family would be. Robert and I were ready. We were playing when Ma Gholston asked us to go into the corn field and bring her 25 "roastnears". They really were roasting ears, but we never said anything but "roastnears". This was perfect because the corn was between our house and Mrs. Ozell's!

We carefully got a basket for the corn and gently placed the egg in the bottom. Into the corn patch we disappeared and reappeared standing directly in front of Mochie's barn! All we had to do was cross the road; walk around the milking parlor and into the hallway where the orange crates hung. Of the six, there were hens in four of the boxes. We carefully placed the "magic egg" in one of the empty crates and scampered back across the road and into the corn field. In short order, we had twenty-five superb "roastnears" and made our way back to the house, shucked the corn and delivered it to Ma's kitchen. Not one adult knew that we had been in Moochie's barn. Why should they?

About two o'clock, Aunt B called Mrs. Ozell and invited them to come for watermelon and ice-cream, just neighbors enjoying fun, food, and fellowship. Somewhere around four-thirty, Mochie said, "We better go and tend to things." "Tend to things" was a phrase used to mean farm chores such as, feeding the chickens, gathering the eggs, milking the cows and slopping the hogs.

Robert Edd and I allowed time for them to get home and change clothes. Earlier, when they came to visit they were still in their Sunday best, and we knew they wouldn't 'tend to things' in those clothes. Then, we playfully ambled into the corn field. Once in, we went up a row as fast as possible. It was so hot, and that corn was sticky. Being encased in corn was a weird feeling, but we were on a mission. Soon we were out of the corn and close to the spot where we had emerged earlier in the day, this time minus an egg.

We stayed very close to the corn for fear that Mr. Mochie or Mrs. Ozell would see us. It got hotter and hotter. We thought about that cold lemonade and watermelon. Then, finally we saw her! Mrs. Ozell had on her work dress and a bibbed apron over it. She was headed to the barn to gather eggs! Joy, Joy!

We could see directly into the hallway of the barn. Quiet as church mice, we watched as Mrs. Ozell pulled the bottom of her apron up to form a pouch. She stepped to the first crate and took out an egg. On to the second one and there were two eggs. The third crate held one egg, and now she was reaching into the fourth crate that had the "magic egg". Would she notice the writing? We held our breathes.

Suddenly, she pulled that egg close to her face. She seemed stunned. She turned it as best she could with her right hand as her left hand held the apron pouch together. Then, as if it were dynamite, she quickly put it back into the crate and just as quickly deposited the other fresh eggs in the crate beside her.

Now, with both hands free she again picked up the 'magic egg'. She held it in her left hand and with her apron tried to erase the message. It would not erase. She realized that it was permanent. "What was happening?" she thought. Mr. Mochie was in the pasture driving the cows to the milk parlor for the evening milking. She had to find somebody. We watched as she quickly forgot the other eggs and went promptly into the house. Robert Edd and I went as quickly into my house. No one was home, thank goodness. Mama, Daddy, and Keylon were still at Ma's & Pa's enjoying the 4th of July celebration.

Our phone was one of eight on what was called a "party line". Four rings were heard on one half the lines and four were heard on the other half. Our ring was one long and one short; Ma and Pa's ring was two shorts and Moochie's and Ozell's was one long.

Mrs. Ozell did exactly what we thought she would do. She immediately called her mother. They lived about a quarter of a mile apart. We gently raised the phone's receiver and heard her exclain that she needed to meet her immediately on Dugger Bridge. The old wooden bridge was about half way between their houses.

With haste, Mrs. Ozell came out her front door and began to walk down the dusty country road. Robert Edd and I trailed her through Daddy's pasture.

When the two women were in the middle of the bridge, Robert Edd and I climbed up to hide beside the bridge so we could see them but not be seen. By now, tears were streaming down Mrs. Ozell's face, and her Mama kept asking her what was wrong. From her apron pocket she produced the magic egg.

"Oh Ozell, where did you get this?" Her Mama asked.

"It was in my hen nest, Mama. The world is ending. That's what God's telling me."

"Ozell, child, God is using you to let the world know." Her mom exclaimed.

As they cried, we laughed. They were loud, we were quiet. This was the best trick ever!!

Then we heard a truck coming. It stopped. I heard a familiar voice. Mr. Houston Grissom said, "Ozell, what's wrong?"

"Houston, look what was in my hen nest!" Carefully, she handed it to him. Stunned he turned the motor off his 1955 Ford. There was no conversation for the longest time.

Then, he said, "Ozell, get in and I'll take you to town. We got to find Walter Anderson." (Mr. Anderson was editor of the Baldwyn News.) It was a weekly paper that was published on

Wednesdays, but in the country, we got ours on Thursday. "He can take a picture of this," Houston said, "and alert everybody in Wednesday's paper."

Suddenly, I felt sick. The fun was gone, and I had no time to think. I knew if the egg inscribed with **"God Shall Return"** appeared in the newspaper, I was dead. I climbed as quickly as I could up the gravel embankment with Robert Edd behind me.

It was time to come clean. Totally clean! At that moment, my main objective was to keep the picture of the "magic egg" out of the newspaper.

"It was just a joke" I said. "We made it with Robert's chemistry set." None of them thought it was funny nor did my Mama or Daddy.

I never cared much for chemistry after that.

What's in the Well

Mama's parents, Ma and Big Daddy Butler lived in the Friendship Community. It was about four miles from our house in Pratt to theirs. The house had big rooms and a front porch that ran the width of the house. This house burned when I was eight and they built a much smaller house. (Joe and Joan Blasingame live there now having completed an addition to the house several years ago.)

Ma Butler kept what was called a 'swept yard'. There was no grass in the front and she swept it clean more than once a day. My job when I was there was to keep the chicken feathers picked up. That yard was an extension of her house, and she wanted both to be very clean at all times. One would never convince Ma Butler that cleanliness was not scripturally taught to be next to Godliness.

Ma Butler's mama was Pinkie Herring Young, we called her Mammie. She lived beside and just back of Ma and Big Daddy with her son, Arnold Lee and her daughter, Brevard Bailey. Brevard's daughter, Belle, also lived there. Mammie's house was small but comfortable. The outhouse (toilet) was across the drive that led to Uncle Leroy's and Aunt Susie's house. Mama and Susie were twins and had one older sister, Tannis.

Mammie's front porch was low to the ground with a brown bench and several chairs. Next to the front door there was a small wooden table that held the water bucket. Just above the bucket, on a nail, hung a dipper. Any time we wanted a drink of water we simply took down the dipper and helped ourselves. When company came, Mammie would send one of the adults to draw a bucket of fresh water. Her well was just to the west of her house and such wonderful, cold water on a hot summer day was always there!

Children weren't allowed near the well for two reasons. One, Mammie said, was because we might fall in, and secondly, we might accidently let something fall into the well.

How special and grown up I felt the first time Mammie asked me if I wanted to go to the well with her. Why, I could not have been more honored if I had been asked to lead the singing at Friendship Baptist Church! Mammie was trusting me to go to her well!

She was very short and very rotund. It seemed to take her an eternity to get out of her chair on the east end of the porch and walk down to the west end and get the water bucket. Finally, we stepped off the porch and toward the well.

Literally, Mammie wasn't more than five feet tall and figuratively, I felt ten feet tall as we walked the few steps to the well. Once there I was mesmerized by the ritual. First, she took a small brush that hung on the post which supported the covering that was two or three feet above the well curb. The well curb was about three feet tall, round with a very thick, heavy wooden cover. The top of the cover was square but underneath, it was perfectly round and fit exactly into the well opening. I remember Mammie having a very difficult time removing the lid. I didn't dare try to help, in part because she said, "stand back," and in part because I was watching the ritual.

Before removing the wooden lid, she used the small brush and brushed the entire top. I didn't see a thing, but I didn't question her procedure either. The entire time she brushed she told me repeatedly, "What's in the well will come up in the water bucket."

Once she had swept to her satisfaction, she hung the small brush back on the nail. Now, she placed her short, stubby fingers under the wooden lid and began to lift. Up an inch, then down. She would work to get a better grip and strain with all her might. Now it seemed to lift about six, maybe eight, or ten inches and then back down.

"Mammie, can I help you?" I was as tall as she was and probably stronger. Four hands underneath seemed twice as good to me.

She thought and said, "Let me see your hands. You holding anything?"

I stretched my hands out and said, "No ma'am, nothing."

"Well you better not drop anything in this well' cause I'm telling you it'll come up in the bucket, and it will ruin the water. Do you hear me?"

I just nodded that I understood, and she motioned for me to lift. Together we got the heavy wooden corner back on the curb by about six to eight inches. She then motioned for me to back up a bit and she moved the lid to allow ample space for the bucket. She secured the bucket to the rope and handed it to me. "Let it down gently. If a wind blows, stop and I'll put the lid on, we can't get no dirt or trash in the well. It'll ruin the water." And, for added emphasis she said, "What's in the well, will always come up in the bucket."

"Yes ma'am," I said and began to lower the bucket as meticulously as if I had been performing brain surgery.

In a while, I heard and felt the bucket as it touched the water. "Give it just enough rope to get the bucket full," she said.

I felt the bucket fill and said, "Mammie, I believe it's full."

"Well, draw it up slow and easy." I did just as she said.

The bucket reached the top of the well curb and she took over. Mammie brought the bucket of cold water out, sat it on the curb, and together we replaced the heavy lid.

"Good work," Mammie said. "We got a bucket of cold water and ain't no trash or dirt in the well. Come on and help me carry this to the porch. You can drink the first dipper full if you want to."

A rite of passage and that cold water was so good. I can taste it now! Throughout life I have learned so much from Mammie's teachings. What is in our well (heart, soul, and spirit) will come up in our buckets (attitudes, work ethics, and treatment of others).

Linda Gholston

Hobos and Pies

In the 1950s my world was so very small. It consisted of our farm, a weekly visit to Ma and Big Daddy's house in the Friendship Community, and an occasional "trip to town" as we called it. This meant going to Baldwyn which was about six miles from the farm. Perhaps twice a year there would be a trip to Tupelo.

Long days of riding my stick horse, making mud pies, and running field to field as the adults worked, filled the months of spring, summer and fall. Winter days were by the big roaring fire watching Ma and Pa Gholston play dominos. They were both very skilled, and the math emphasis didn't hurt me at all.

Because Mama and Daddy were constantly busy on the farm I spent most of my waking hours with Ma Gholston, Sophronia Alice Philpot Gholston. She was the warmest, kindest, most generous person I ever knew. Up before daylight, she cooked her wonderful biscuits along with eggs, gravy and farm raised pork for the family. After washing all the dishes, she would begin immediately on dinner. (We called the midday meal dinner and the night meal was supper.) Dinner would consist of fresh or home canned vegetables, cornbread, sometimes chicken and always one of her famous desserts. Every day she made a cake, pie, or cobbler.

The west side of Ma's kitchen had a window with a window ledge. When she baked something and wanted it to cool a bit, she would cover it with a dish cloth and set it on the ledge of the open window. I remember one day she and I peeled fresh peaches from Pa's orchard. She made a crust and an hour later took a steaming hot peach pie from the oven. She told me that she would put it on the ledge of the open window as she planned to use fresh cream from yesterday's milking and have whipped cream to top the pie.

For the next couple of hours, I tried, as best I could, to ride my stick horse, but my mind was on the peach pie. Finally, I got in the big swing on the front porch and fell asleep. As Mama, Daddy, Uncle Bulich, Pa Gholston, and others came from the fields, I came out of my deep sleep and was ready to eat!

Once we were stuffed with her good corn, butter beans, squash, tomatoes, cucumbers, and cornbread she asked, "Who wants peach pie with fresh whipped cream". Of course, all of us did. Ma got up from the table in the dining room, walked into the kitchen and over to the ledge. She held out both hands to grasp the pie plate, but the ledge was empty.

We all groaned and moaned. Pa said, "Them hobos will steal you blind." It was not uncommon to see hobos traveling on foot at that time throughout the community.

I remember Ma Gholston saying. "Fate, we are full. He was hungry. I just wish he had asked. I would have given him the pie." ("Fate" was the name Ma Gholston called Pa Gholston whose full name was Marcus Dablin de Lafayette Gholston.)

Linda Gholston

Mourning and Forgiving

I hope everyone who reads this has a 'Ma Gholston' in their memory. Should you not, I will gladly share mine. She grew up in the late 1800s in hard times. Her parents were share croppers in and around Prentiss County. With four sons and two daughters, they decided to go to Oklahoma by covered wagon. While there in 1893, another daughter, Maggie, was born in Indian Territory.

Great grandpa Philpot (Samuel Donald) and the boys secured work on a ranch and Oklahoma became home. Then Grandpa became ill and died in 1894. My great grandmother, Mariah Dexter Camp Philpot, and her children, including baby Maggie, headed back to Prentiss County, Mississippi in the covered wagon after a son was accused of murder.

The story was that the ranch owner's son killed a man but was laying the blame on the "hired hand". So, as a young teenager, Saphronia Alice, her siblings, and mother came back to northeast Mississippi since Ma's brother was "the hired hand".

It would be several years later that she (Saphronia Alice) would meet and marry Marcus Dablin de 'Lafayette Gholston. He and his daddy, B Gholston (Nathaniel Bonaparte), had bought land in the Pratt Community and built a house in the late 1890s. This house is where Ma and Pa came on their wedding day and never lived anywhere else. To say our roots run deep is an understatement!

Ma and Pa Gholston had four sons: Edwone, Bulich, Marvin and Douglas (my daddy) and one daughter, Lula B. World War II happened, and all four boys wanted to do their patriotic duty and serve. My daddy, Douglas, reported to Camp Shelby, Mississippi. Due to scarring seen on his chest x-ray, he was sent home for fear he had tuberculosis. He had suffered scarring from severe childhood asthma.

My daddy lived his entire life regretting that he could not serve his country, but he came to realize how much he was needed on the farm during those years.

So, my grandparents had three sons fighting in World War II simultaneously. Uncle Edd was in England, Uncle Bulich in France, and Uncle Marvin in Japan. Uncle Marvin was just older than Daddy and married my Mama's sister, Tannis Butler.

Perhaps this story told to me by Daddy embodies Ma Gholston best....

Uncle Marvin and another soldier were in a foxhole. Gunfire was heavy. A Japanese soldier jumped into the foxhole and stabbed Uncle Marvin in the chest. He died instantly.

Daddy said the entire community grieved with them. They all were heart broken. One son killed, and two others had fought. Uncle Edd was home, but Uncle Bulich wasn't discharged when the word of Uncle Marvin's death came.

Before Uncle Marvin's body was returned for burial, a letter came addressed to Mrs. Sophronia A. Gholston. It was from the soldier who shared the foxhole with Uncle Marvin. He concluded his letter with:

Mrs. Gholston, I want you to know I got the Jap who got Marvin.

Daddy said Ma folded the letter, returned it to the envelope and said, "I'm so sorry. Now, two mothers are grieving."

Only the love of God could enable Ma Gholston to say and mean that. After all these years, she continues to be my model for living. I fall short, but can say unequivocally, I am a better person for having known and been loved by Sophronia Alice Philpot Gholston.

Linda Gholston

Looking Back

When I was about four or five years old, Pa Gholston, in his early seventies, made a monumental decision. He told my Daddy and Uncle Bulich that he was finished with corn, cotton, cattle and hay bailing. He would spend the morning working in the garden, orchard, and truck patch. After dinner, he was going to do nothing but sit under the shade tree and whittle.

I loved Pa Gholston being "semi-retired" – all I knew was during good weather he would whittle, and I would play. A great combination!

Every afternoon at three o'clock we walked to Mr. Boyce Norton's store and reached into his ice-cold drink box and had a 'Coke-Cola'. He spent a dime on two Coke-Colas every day! Then we would journey back to the farm and chat.

One afternoon Mr. Crabtree came by. He lived somewhere north of Baldwyn and had spent a few years in Illinois working for an automobile manufacturer. Pa said, "He stayed up north just long enough to get that Yankee brogue." He did talk funny. Didn't sound anything like us or our neighbors.

I remember he was an extremely tall, thin man who always had on black trousers, a white shirt, and a thin black tie. I never cared for him, as he interrupted our play and really acted like I didn't exist.

But this particular afternoon when he stopped his car and got out he seemed especially chipper. Pa said his usual, "Get out and sit awhile".

Mr. Crabtree abruptly said, "Fate, I don't have time to sit. I came to show you my brand-new car. Brand new! Nothing second hand about this jewel." As he talked he was using the sleeve of his dingy white shirt to rub some dust from the fender.

"Fate, this is the third one of these ever to be in Lee County and the first in Prentiss County. Ain't she a beaut?" It was a surf blue 1952 Buick Roadmaster. He said his wife chose the color, and it was very rare.

Pa stopped whittling, nodded his approval but Mr. Crabtree said, "Fate, you ever been inside a brand spanking new automobile?"

"No, can't say as I have."

"Well, come and just sit in it, feel the genuine leather seats and smell that new car smell, Fate."

Pa was a tall man and much thicker than Mr. Crabtree. He unfolded himself from his cane-bottomed chair, stood up, walked to the car and looked inside. "Mighty nice, mighty nice."

"Fate, this automobile has something I guarantee you ain't never seen."

"What is it?" Pa asked

"A glare-free rear view mirror, Look right up there on the windshield, Fate. I can see where I've been with no glare," Mr. Crabtree said with great emotion and in an extremely high-pitched voice. "Cost me a right smart of extra money, but I got it Fate!"

Didn't make sense to me and I could tell it didn't make a lot to Pa either. Mr. Crabtree leaned ever so gently against his car and for thirty-minutes he told Pa all about his new ride. It was after three when he left, and I couldn't wait to head to Mr. Boyce's for our Coke-Colas.

As we walked I heard Pa grumbling. I think he wasn't any more impressed with Mr. Crabtree's purchase than I was.

About a month later Pa's brother, Uncle Sydney came to visit. He was a wise, well-read man and I loved just listening to him. His voice was soothing, and his coming to visit was always a pleasant surprise.

As he and Pa talked, Uncle Sydney said, "Mr. Crabtree wrecked his new car yesterday."

Pa asked, "Was he hurt?"

"No, I don't reckon he was," Uncle Syd said.

Pa chuckled, "Probably looking in that glare-free rear view mirror."

After a while, Uncle Sydney left. I was playing in the dirt and Pa was whittling. We were both quiet, but I could tell he was thinking.

In a bit he said, "I don't know about them no glare rear-view mirrors. They may be a standard in vehicles of the future. Don't ever spend a lot of your time Sister, looking at where you have been. Spend most of your time looking at where you're going."

Good advice. Has served me well.

Sowing and Reaping

Late summer was an interesting time on the farm. All the spring gardens had been picked and eaten or put up for winter. As Pa Gholston said, "The crops were laid by". That simply meant corn, cotton and soy beans had been harvested and hay baled for the cold winter months. There was just a very short growing season left and it was time for the "truck patch". This would be a few select vegetables that we would grow, harvest, eat on in the late fall, or harvest and dry and store in the floor of the well house for winter.

The shelves in the well house and Ma's pantry were full of jars canned from the spring garden. If there was any space available, we might can a few more jars of peas and beans but they would primarily be allowed to dry on the vine. Then we would pick and shell them. Shelling dried peas and butter-beans was the worse task of fall. Ma would pick the vegetables, shell them, clean off any debris and put them in white flour sacks. The sacks would be tightly secured with strips of material and kept in cool, dry places. Then, as needed, a mess of peas or beans would be removed, and the sack tied and placed back where it was kept.

These dried vegetables and fruits would see us through many a cold winter day.

Daddy and Uncle Bulich would prepare about four to six long rows for fall peas. Then they would put the "hoppers" on the Ferguson tractor and plant peas. So, each year there would be only one variety of peas in the truck patch. There would be two rows of butterbeans, some potatoes, and late squash (winter squash). No one in our family cared for pumpkin, so when the other truck patches looked festive for fall, ours did not. Pa said we weren't going to raise food we wouldn't eat. He did however plant a few gourds each year for birdhouses in the spring and summer.

The ground was prepared for the truck patch in mid-summer of 1953. I was going to be six in October. Daddy said at noon one day, "Linda, do you want to choose the peas for the truck patch?"

Wow! Did I! I must be about grown if Daddy is trusting me with such a major decision. I didn't hesitate. "Yes, Sir I do, Daddy!"

"Ok, what will it be?" (I've thought for several years he knew my choice and it would be his, too!)

"Purple Hull! I love purple hull peas. The pot licker is purple, and it makes your cornbread purple. Can I really, Daddy? Can I?"

"Yes, I'll tell Bulich to get the seed peas out, fill the hopper and in no time at all we will have ourselves some good fall purple hull peas."

Uncle Bulich went into the house and asked Ma Gholston where the seed peas were. She told him the seeds were in the well house; on the shelf to his right would be purple hulls and on the shelf to his left would be Mississippi Silvers. How could anyone confuse those instructions?

As Uncle Bulich was finishing attaching the hoppers and making sure every part of the tractor was greased and ready to go, Curtis Glenn pulled up in his truck and wanted Uncle Bulich to listen to the engine. They were great friends and Uncle Bulich was happy to help Curtis. After listening intently for a few minutes, he felt there was trash in the carburetor, so he removed it, cleaned it and reattached it.

Finally, Uncle Bulich went to the well house and got the sack of peas. We watched as he planted those seeds in that rich dirt. Then he planted butter beans and removed the hoppers.

Boy! In no time those pea plants were sticking their heads through the ground. Daddy said, "perfect stand!" Then they began to flower. Within a few days the little pea pods began to form. Over a period of time they were about half grown, and peas were forming inside. The only problem was there was no purple. The flowers weren't purple and the peas' shells weren't purple. They were whitish-silver. Daddy went to the well house and realized that somehow Uncle Bulich had picked up the Mississippi Silvers. The purple hulls remained in their flour sack on the shelf to the right. Unplanted.

Daddy dreaded telling me. He milked the cows, we ate supper and he said, "Come and walk out to the truck patch with me".

It was a strange request but the invitation to go anywhere with my Daddy was all I needed. Out the door we went. I was barefoot, dirty from the day, and tired. But put me with my Daddy and all was right with the world. I heard him say to Mama, "We'll be back d'rectly". (Which meant soon.)

He talked about the good crops we had been blessed with, the hay in the barn and the calves in the pasture. I just inhaled his scent of sweat, dirt, grease, milk, and hog slop. Pretty sure it was bad, but smelled wonderful to me.

Soon we stood in the peas. He picked one and began to open it, although the peas weren't nearly mature. "What color are these peas?" Daddy asked.

"They are green now Daddy, but they will be purplish when they are ready to pick." I said with authority.

"No, no they won't, Hon. They are Mississippi Silvers. Uncle Bulich picked up the wrong sack. He feels really bad."

Boy! Did I pitch a fit! Nothing was more important to me than food and I loved Purple Hull Peas. This was my first time to choose and Uncle Bulich had ruined it.

Daddy patiently let me cry and fuss. After a short hissy fit, he said, "Dry those tears. What is done is done. He feels bad about it. Do you understand me, Linda Joy?"

I sniffled and rubbed my runny nose and said "Yes, Sir".

He picked me up in his strong arms and walked to the end of the truck patch. A sassafras tree was there, and gently Daddy sat down beside me.

Slowly and with a little sadness in his voice he said, "The Bible says we reap what we sow. You see those rows over there?"

"Yes, Sir."

"We planted peanuts, and we're going to dig peanuts." He moved his fingers a bit and said, "See those plants."

"Yes, Sir. They're sweet potatoes."

"Right! And we'll dig sweet potatoes."

On these six long rows you and I wanted to pick Purple Hulls, but we will pick and shell dried Mississippi Silvers because that's what got planted there," Daddy said.

"Yes, Sir, but I don't like'em much Daddy. You told me to pick and I picked Purple Hulls." My heart was breaking.

"I know that, but Uncle Bulich, by mistake, got the wrong sack of seed. Now we can cry and fuss til dark, but those are going to be Mississippi Silver peas. Understand?"

"Yes, Sir, I do."

"As you live your life, you'll plant lots of seeds. The Bible won't be wrong. You will reap what you sow."

"Well, Daddy, I ain't sowing Mississippi Silvers."

"Well, Linda, I'm not talking peas. I'm talking about how you treat others, how kind your heart is and the good you do. Always try to plant good seeds, will you?"

"Yes, Sir, I will. I'm sleepy, Daddy. Can we go to the house? I'll eat ''em' Mississippi Silvers and make sure Uncle Bulich sees me. Ok, Daddy?"

"Ok, that's my girl."

Salvation

I always loved going to church. As a child we didn't go regularly, but on the Sundays we did, I loved it. Sometimes we would go to Friendship Baptist, sometimes to Pratt Christian and sometimes to "Pinhook". (The real name is East Mount Zion Baptist)

Pa Gholston always told me that the Pratt community was named for Mr. Tom Pratt, but that people called the west side "Frog level" and the east side "Pinhook". The story was that a new family settled on the west side and the first night the man went out to milk their only cow, a frog jumped into his milk bucket. He went in the house and told his wife, "we have moved to Frog level"! Pa said the road on the east side of Pratt had such a sharp curve they called it 'Pinhook'. I don't know if these stories are true or not, but they were "gospel truth" to me.

I recall different preachers at the three churches. At "Pin hook" I remember Brother Wilson. He was a soft spoken, mild mannered man who could quote scripture like nobody I knew. One-time Mama invited the Wilson's to have Sunday dinner with us. I remember she had fried chicken, home-made biscuits and gravy and banana pudding. The Wilsons loved Mama's cooking. When she served the banana pudding, Mrs. Wilson asked,

"Trixie, you got any 'yuyons'?"

"Yes, I do. Sorry I didn't slice one. It won't take but a jiffy," Mama said.

"Well, 'naner puddin' just ain't the same without a slice of yuyon," Mrs. Wilson proclaimed.

I saw Mama and Daddy look at each other like they might throw up. Brother Wilson kept his head down and chomped on another chicken leg.

Mrs. Wilson was a big woman. She took her saucer and filled it full of Mama's famous banana pudding and reached for a slice of onion. She finished both in record time. Not to be out done, I said, "Mama I want onion with my puddin', too." She looked disgusted but let me have it.

Brother Colson was a favorite of mine at Pratt, Brothers Digby and Davidson at Friendship and as a teen I dearly loved Brother Phillips at East Mount Zion. The Bible and all of these pastors along with others influenced and helped mold my beliefs.

When I was fourteen, I was not by any stretch a Bible scholar. I did know that Christ had died for my sins, and that I had not accepted His gift of salvation. I would think about it occasionally and then try to dismiss it. I would go to church and hold the back of the pew in front of me during the song of invitation. No doubt, God's spirit was leading me to repentance and acceptance, but I wasn't being obedient.

In June, Daddy announced that we were going to Uncle Edd's for two days. We never went anywhere. First reason, we milked cows twice a day and second reason, my daddy was a 'home body'.

Uncle Bulich and Curtis Glenn had agreed to "tend to things" Daddy said. That meant milk the cows, feed the chickens and slop the hogs.

I couldn't believe it! We were going to Starkville for two whole days! Mama found a 'cardboard' box for us to pack our clothes.

Then Daddy asked, "Know what we are going to do?"

"No Sir" I answered.

"We are taking Edd's boat to Sardis. The bream will be beddin' and we can catch the limit."

My unsaved heart hit rock bottom. Tomorrow morning before day's light we were leaving our home to get in a boat. 'I might drown' was all I could think.

"Daddy, how big is that Sardis Lake?" (Like it mattered)

"Big. Out in the middle you can't see the shore." I about died.

"Is it really deep?"

"Over forty feet in places."

"Will we go out that deep?"

"Oh sure. You know them big blue gills you like to catch at the Sportsman's Lake, well these are bigger." The thought of fish, boats and trips made me sick to my stomach.

I went to my room and got on my knees in front of the two windows that faced north. I don't remember the exact words, but I gave my heart to Jesus. At that time, I understood very little about His Lordship, but I knew that His shed blood covering my sins was how I became "an adopted child of God."

I remember climbing into that boat and Uncle Edd cranking that motor and us riding out to the middle of Sardis Lake. I still didn't want to drown, but knew if I did that Jesus was now my personal Savior.

That was more than fifty-five years ago and to this day, the best decision I have ever made.

Scotty Kim

When I was eight, a puppy appeared at our house. We lived so near the old wooden bridge it wasn't that unusual for us to find unwanted puppies or kittens that people had discarded near the water. This puppy was tiny, a cream color with a few darker spots. I had my boxer, Buster Brown, but he was big and grown and my major protection. After lots of begging and pleading, Daddy said we could keep the puppy.

I named her Scotty Kim. Where that name came from I don't have a clue. She was a little 'Heinz 57' variety but mostly feist. We bathed her and got her ready to be a part of our family. No dogs were allowed to sleep inside so Scotty Kim bunked with Buster at night.

Now, she only lacked one thing. I wanted her tail bobbed. Buster's was. Daddy explained to me that boxers had their tails bobbed as puppies, but feists were meant to have long tails. I had never had a dog with a long tail and I didn't intend to start.

I knew by eight years old how far I could push Daddy. I had pushed to the limit. It was July, hot as could be, he was baling hay and milking cows and Mama was very pregnant. Trying to convince her was like convincing a stump, and she told me one afternoon, "If you mention bob tailing that dog again your Daddy is going to take it to town and give it to some child who knows feists don't have bobbed tails. Do you hear me, Linda Joy?"

"Yes, Mama"

"Do you understand me?"

"Yes, Mama"

After Daddy finished milking he asked if we wanted to go see Ma and Big Daddy. Did that lift my spirits! "Can I take my new puppy to show them?"

"Yes, I reckon so. Your Big Daddy may make a squirrel dog out of her." Daddy answered.

That pleased me, that Scotty Kim might have a purpose like Buster. Mama and Daddy depended on him for protection and he did his job well! One day, Mrs. Ozell McCarthy was going to whip Larry in the back yard and Buster ran her into the house kicking and screaming. Larry and I laughed, but didn't let her see us!

When we got out of the truck at Ma's and Big's, Big was sitting on the back porch. He operated a roadgrader for Lee County. The roads were dirt and gravel and Big Daddy kept them smooth, no pot holes in his roads. He was a man who took great pride in his work. When he wasn't working, he was hunting or fishing. Big Daddy trained birddogs for people constantly.

In fact, he had just trained two dogs for Dr. Stokes before he came to Big's and Ma's house to deliver 'a baby' in March 1927. During the delivery, he realized there were two babies. He handed Big Daddy the first little girl and said, "Here's Susie" and in about two minutes he said, "And here's Trixie." Even though their names were legally Vera and Era, my mama (Trixie) and her twin, my aunt Susie always were called Dr. Stokes bird dogs' names!

Big Daddy liked Scotty Kim immediately. He held her and inspected her as if she was a rare jewel. "You've got a fine one here, Sister. I may borrow her to hunt."

"You can Big. You can."

Mama, Daddy and Ma Butler had disappeared into the house. Ma said she had been frying peach pies and that's all it took for them to disappear.

"Can I ask you something, Big?"

"Sure, you can."

"Well, I want Scotty Kim to be bobtailed like Buster, but Mama and Daddy said if I mention it again they will give her away."

He held my puppy and felt of her tail as if he knew magic. Finally, he said, "You really want her bobtailed?"

"Yes Sir, I do Big."

"Well, we can do it, but you can't say a word to your Mama and Daddy. Do you promise?"

"Yes Sir, I do."

"Ok. It'll take two or three weeks, but I swear it'll work."

"Ok. Let's do it." My eyes were wide, and my heart was beating fast.

"Now, Sister, you can't tell your Mama and Daddy. But after it's done, ain't no way they can put it back on. Come on to the shed."

He carried Scotty Kim and I followed. Ma Butler hollered out the kitchen window, "Baby Girl, do you want a fried pie?"

"Later, Ma, I sure do."

That should have let them know that Big and I were up to something!

In the shed he opened his tool box and found a compartment full of rubber bands. He was half talking to me and half to himself, "Here's a short one that's strong enough to do the trick." He wrapped it as many times as he could around Scotty's tail about three-fourths way up. "This will hold. Don't mess with it and, don't you tell your Mama and Daddy."

"No Sir, Big. Thank you. I love you!" I went immediately into the house and began to 'inhale' fried peach pies. I was one happy young'un. If Big said it will work, it will work!!

About two weeks later, Mama was sitting on the front porch. It was the end of July. She and Ma Butler had been canning the last few tomatoes of summer. Ma told Mama to go rest, and she would clean the kitchen. Mama sat in a straight-backed chair and leaned back against the house. There was a breeze and she said it felt so good to her. I was sitting on the front door step.

Buster and Scotty Kim came scampering across the front yard. Just as they got in front of Mama, Scotty Kim's tail fell off! Mama began to scream. The dogs ran. I looked at the ground.

Ma Butler ran to the door, flung it open and in a panic asked, "Are you in labor?"

"No, Mama, NO – Worse than that."

"What's wrong?"

"I'm having a stroke."

"A stroke?"

"Yes, I just saw a dog's tail fall off." Ma Butler started to cry. She ran to get wet towels. Mama was hysterical.

"Go catch that dog and bring her here", Mama said.

"Yes, Ma'am"

Around the house I went. I picked up Scotty Kim and sure enough her tail was gone! Hallelujah and Oh My!

I carried her to Mama and said, "See Mama. You're not having a stroke. Her tail is gone."

About that time, Ma was back with wet towels. She looked at Scotty Kim's bobbed tail and said, "That Noel Butler. Ought to be ashamed of 'hisself'. I know he 'done' it. Seen him do it a hundred times. Wait til I get home. This will mark the baby as sure as everything and it will be his fault."

What did 'mark a baby' mean? I didn't know and wasn't going to ask. I had my bobtailed puppy and on October 16^{th,} I got my "unmarked" baby!

Revival and Dry Cleaning

Mama's twin sister, Susie, married LeRoy Blasingame. Uncle LeRoy was a lot of fun and I loved being at their house. Their daughter, Becky, is eleven months older than me so we grew up playing together.

Uncle LeRoy was the body shop foreman at Henderson Chevrolet in Baldwyn. People would bring their vehicles of all makes and models to him for repair. It always amazed me that he went to work at seven and was home by a quarter after five each day except on Saturday; he was off the whole afternoon. Growing up I didn't understand the difference in farming hours and business hours.

When I was almost ten, Mama decided that we (She, Keylon and I) would go spend the first week of August with Aunt Susie, Uncle LeRoy, and Becky. This was revival at Friendship Baptist Church. I was so excited! Daddy would come for the night service when he could, but we would be there for the morning and evening services!

Also, I was excited because Uncle Bulich had taught me a trick to play on Uncle LeRoy. I had practiced and was ready. It would happen on Tuesday because that's the day "the dry cleaning came." Back then, the local cleaner ran a route and would pick up and deliver clothes that had to be dry cleaned. This kept farmers and others from having to make a trip to town.

Funny, I don't remember the dry-cleaning truck ever stopping at our house, but it stopped at Aunt Susie's every Tuesday. They obviously had more store-bought clothes than we did, and even though I don't remember for sure, I suspect Uncle LeRoy's uniforms were laundered. He always looked sharp in those navy pants and shirts. I marveled that his name was just above the pocket on each shirt! Mighty special!

On this Tuesday we were up and ready for the revival service long before ten o'clock. We walked to Friendship Baptist Church, which was less than one-half mile from their house. Keylon was just ten months old, so all the adults took turns 'toting' him. Those who didn't get a turn going, got theirs coming back.

We got home, ate and Becky and I started playing. About two o'clock, here came the dry-cleaning truck. My trick was working so far.

Wayne Stone got out with the laundry, as Aunt Susie gave him the bag she had to send for cleaning. He told us all good-bye and was on his way. Nobody, but Uncle Bulich and I knew what was coming when Uncle LeRoy got home.

About quarter past five I saw his car turn into the driveway. He parked and came into the house. Mama and Aunt Susie were busy getting clothes ready for the evening service. We wouldn't have to walk, because Uncle LeRoy was there with the car.

So, he came in, took his shoes off and sat down to rest awhile before supper. I sat down on the couch beside him and made sure everybody else was out of hearing range.

"Uncle LeRoy, if you'll give me a quarter I'll tell you what Wayne Stone said to Aunt Susie this afternoon."

He bit! Quick as a flash he reached into his left pants' pocket and brought out a hand full of change. With the fore finger and thumb of his right hand he picked out a shiny quarter and handed it to me.

"What did he say?"

"You got any laundry today, Susie."

He looked dumbfounded, but I had him. Just as I was admiring my quarter, Daddy walked in. He had 'tended to things', got dressed for church and had come for supper.

Uncle LeRoy said, "Douglas, you need to make Linda Joy give me back my quarter."

"How did she get it?" Daddy asked.

Uncle LeRoy told him the whole story.

Daddy chuckled and said, "I heard Bulich telling her that prank. Sounds like to me you fell for it, LeRoy. The quarter is hers."

I love my Daddy!

My Sister and Me

Mama and Daddy were married on July 4, 1945. He was twenty; she was eighteen. Brother Parker performed the ceremony with them sitting in the back seat of Curtis Glenn's car and the preacher on his knees in the front seat. Why in the car and not in the church, I don't know.

I do know that Mama wanted Brother Parker to perform the ceremony because she, Aunt Susie, and Aunt Tannis sang as a trio and often sang for Brother Parker at his church and in revival services. Some Saturdays they would go to the radio station in Booneville to sing for a program where he preached. This was quite a distance to travel. Big Daddy never owned a vehicle, but I remember Mama saying that Rivers Martin took them most Saturdays. After Aunt Tannis and Uncle Marvin began to date, he would sometimes borrow a car and take them.

Mama and Daddy lived with Ma and Pa Gholston until one of Pa's two share-cropper houses became vacant. We called it the "little red house" because it had red shingles. The house sat behind and to the east of Ma's and Pa's house, probably about two tenths of a mile. It was a very easy walk. The house had one fairly large room with a big, open fireplace on the east end. There was room for a bed, a couch, a rocking chair and straight back chairs that could be used around the fireplace. There was a 'lean-to' at the back that had a wood stove for cooking and a small table with four unmatched chairs. On the west side, a small room no larger than a closet held a number three wash tub for bathing and the chamber pot (our bathroom at night and in bad weather).

The outdoor toilet sat behind and just east of the house. We used corn cobs, old newspapers, and pages from Sears catalogues for toilet paper. The well was a pump with a long handle secured in an underground artesian well. Coldest water ever! It was downhill to the northwest of the house.

The house was nothing more than a shack, and oftentimes rain would be pouring through more places than Mama had pots and pans to catch the water. The cracks in the floor were wide and plentiful so eventually the water got back to the ground.

On Saturday mornings Mama would pull that number three tub out onto the front porch. She would take the water bucket to the well and bring that ice-cold spring fed water until the tub was at least half full. It would sit in the sun all day. Late afternoon she would strip me naked and, into the tub, I'd go with a bar of home-made lye soap. After my bath, she would bathe and then when Daddy finished milking he would bathe. That water was pretty foul, but we were clean and mighty red where that lye soap lathered a bit too long. It's a good thing our house sat far off the road and couldn't easily be seen. In the winter time the only difference in the routine was the tub was pulled into the house close to the open fire place.

In May 1946, Mama and Daddy's first baby was due! Mama had had an uneventful pregnancy and when she went into labor, Daddy got Curtis Glenn to take them to Caldwell Hospital in Baldwyn. They didn't really care if it was a boy or girl, just so it was healthy.

Elizabeth Ann came through the birth canal and went immediately to heaven. A beautiful little girl with a grossly enlarged liver. Ma Gholston would tell me in later years that she was the most beautiful baby she had ever seen. She was buried in a white gown in a white casket. Ma said she had lots of hair with dark, thick ringlets.

In 1946, the thinking was that it was best for a mother not to see her deceased baby. So, they buried Elizabeth Ann with Mama never seeing her. Mama always regretted this, and I do, too. I have witnessed beauty and healing several times as couples have held and loved on their deceased babies. It is a time for bonding and grieving. Mama and Daddy didn't have this.

The most glorious thing is that Mama, Daddy, and Elizabeth Ann are all together now in the presence of Jesus, a reunion that will last for all eternity in perfectly well, glorified bodies.

After losing Elizabeth Ann, Mama and Daddy returned to the "little red house" and continued to work hard on the farm. I don't know how they dealt with their grief as individuals or as a couple. I suspect stoically, without lots of open discussion. Privately.

On October 6, 1947, they returned to Caldwell Hospital for the birth of their second child. Throughout pregnancy Mama had said, if it's another girl, she wanted to name the baby after her childhood friend, Lavata Sue.

As Mama's labor progressed the whole family gathered. There were no sonograms, only a basic stethoscope. Dr. Caldwell told the family, "All I can say is, Trixie is in labor and the baby has a strong heartbeat. We will know shortly. Ya'll pray while I deliver this baby."

Daddy said that time seemed to stand still. He felt it was just yesterday, he had stood in that hallway, waiting. That outcome was not good. He just prayed and tried to keep his mind in the present. To keep his mind occupied he said he thought about shoeing horses, planting peanuts and fishing. Those were things he seldom did, so they took a lot of concentration.

Finally, Dr. Caldwell came out and said, "Douglas, you've got a girl! She's breathing and seems just fine. I'd say you've got you a hand to milk the cows. She's hungry and screaming her head off!"

Ma Butler and Ma Gholston cried with delight and thanksgiving. Daddy calmly said to the nurse, "Can we fill out the papers for the birth certificate?"

"You want to do that before Trixie is fully awake?" she asked.

"Yes ma'am, if I can," Daddy answered quietly.

"Ok. First name", she asked.

"Linda"

"Middle name?"

Daddy hesitated, "I don't know. Let's just go with Linda Gholston and let me get to the post office."

"Douglas," the nurse said, "every baby deserves a middle name."

My Aunt Tannis was standing nearby and said, "Douglas, it is such a joy for ya'll to finally have a baby, why don't you name her Linda Joy?"

With a sigh of relief, Daddy said, "Yes, Linda Joy. That's it!"

With the form filled out, Daddy walked to the post office. Mama woke up a few hours later to find that she had a healthy baby girl. Not Lavata Sue but Linda Joy! Thanks Mama for birthing me, and thanks Daddy for naming me!

Linda Gholston

My Brother Charlie

When I was six I really wanted Mama to have a baby. She explained to me, more than once, that there would be no more children. After I was born Mama suffered a horrible infection as part of the placenta was not passed. For over two weeks Mama ran an extremely high fever and the doctor really thought she was in danger of dying. With aspirin, penicillin and prayer she pulled through. However, the doctor assured her she had her one and only child.

For months I begged. I loved every baby we saw. I began to ask God to please send me a baby brother or sister. I didn't care which, I just wanted a baby. Mama kept telling me that she couldn't have more children. So, I devised a plan that I thought would work fabulously. We had moved to the house Daddy and Mama built. Daddy went to the saw mill and planed the lumber himself. Mr. Dalton Ray then built the little house. It was small with no indoor bathroom at the time, but it didn't leak, and you couldn't see the ground through the cracks in the floor.

The Mooneyhans lived in the sharecropper house we called "The Taylor House." It was much larger and in better condition than "The Little Red House." I loved the Mooneyhans living there! They had lots of kids, so I always had someone to play with. My favorite was Charlie a boy about my age.

I stopped pestering Mama about a baby. I had Charlie but sometimes I would still ask God for a baby.

We had moved into our new house in October. I was adjusted to the first grade and Charlie and I played until dark every-day. I never dreamed my apple cart could be turned over so quickly.

One night at the supper table Daddy said to Mama, "I got some bad news."

"What's that," she asked.

"The Mooneyhans are moving west of town. Sure do hate to lose them. Old man Mooneyhan said they'd stay til the crops are out. Maybe another week to ten days and we ought to have all the hay in the barn."

I started to cry. "What's wrong?" Daddy asked as he worked mayonnaise into a plate full of peas. Fresh peas, canned peas, dried peas; my daddy covered them with mayonnaise. I like mine like that too!

"I don't want Little Charlie to move. Who will I play with?"

"You'll find somebody," Daddy said as he ate peas and cornbread.

"I hope they are getting a big house," Mama said. "There's so many of them. I don't even know how many kids there is over there, do you?"

"A bunch is all I know," Daddy said as he drank a big swig of cold milk. With a chuckle he said, "Hope they take em all on moving day." He and Mama laughed a little and moved on to other things, but I had planning to do.

The next day was Saturday so Charlie and I could play a long time. When I saw him coming across the pasture I ran out to meet him.

"Charlie, y'all are moving."

"We are? Where?"

"I don't know. West of town is all I know but too far away for us to play." The move didn't seem nearly as painful for Charlie as it was for me.

"Charlie, I don't want you to go."

"I don't neither but reckon I'll have to."

"No, ya don't. You can live with Mama, Daddy and me."

Charlie looked at me rather disgruntled and said, "That ain't gonna happen."

"Yes, it is. Listen to me Charlie and don't tell anybody. Ok?"

"Ok."

"The day your folks pack up the truck you climb that big sweet gum tree over there by ya'lls house. Be quiet. After they leave come down and come to Ma Gholston's."

He nodded but I wasn't so sure.

On Thursday night Daddy said they would finish the hay by dinner on Friday. The Mooneyhans would pack up and leave early Saturday morning.

I went over the plan with Charlie again. Even tho' he said he would do it, I really couldn't tell if Charlie wanted to stay but I wanted it bad enough for both of us.

On Friday night Daddy told Mama that he would milk early Saturday morning and then he and Mr. Clovis Mink were going to the sale barn. It was in Tupelo and the two of them would buy cattle to resell. Daddy was phenomenal with calculations. He could look at a cow, guess within ten pounds her weight and within one or two cents how much she would bring per pound and calculate what she would sell for. He supplemented our income buying and selling cattle.

So, on Saturday I was in the front yard at Ma Gholston's pretending to play but really waiting for this to be the day I got me a brother, Charlie Mooneyhan!

About ten o'clock Pa was in his chair whittling. It was a gorgeous October day. Not too hot; not to cold. We heard the old truck coming from the pasture that led to the Taylor House. It was packed with all the Mooneyhans possessions and kids were all on top of the mattresses, dressers and tables. I looked as best I could but didn't see Charlie. Could the plan be working?

Mr. and Mrs. Mooneyhan waved big as they passed by. They had been over the night before to tell Ma and Pa goodbye so up the long drive the old truck sputtered. Just as they turned on to the main road that truck back fired. I almost jumped out of my skin and Pa just laughed. "You thought they was shooting at us, didn't you, Sister?"

I thought, "Pa, if my plan works, they may." But I stayed quiet and played in the front yard.

It seemed an eternity, but finally I looked down the farm road. Lo and behold Charlie Mooneyhan was skipping along kicking up dust. I ran to meet him. I was so happy! I had me a brother and it wasn't even hard. Charlie seemed melancholy, but I was thrilled.

No sooner we got to the front yard and Ma Gholston called us to dinner. Charlie and I ran into the house like two young puppies going to nurse. Mama came out of the kitchen and said, "Charlie, I thought ya'll left about two hours ago?

"They did, Miss Trixie."

"Well. How come you're still here?"

Charlie just shrugged his shoulders and eyed the table of food like he was starving. "Well climb up and eat", Mama said. We fixed our plates full of vegetables and even had some sliced fall tomatoes. Life just didn't get better. My prayer for a brother had been answered. I thought.

After we ate Ma asked Charlie to take a basket out to the apple tree and bring in enough for two pies. He left, and I said I'd go help him.

"Not so fast," Mama said. "Tell us why Charlie is still here."

"Well, y'all know I been wanting a baby. He ain't no baby but Mama, you and Daddy said they had so many kids they might leave one."

Aunt B said, "Don't say ain't." She knew well as I did that grammar was the least of my worries.

So, I told Mama, Ma, Pa, Uncle Bulich, and Aunt B the whole story. Uncle Bulich laughed, Pa shook his head and the women just kind of stared into space. Finally, Uncle Bulich broke the silence. "When Douglas gets in from the salebarn y'all gonna have to take him west of Baldwyn. Tell him to use my truck."

"What? Take him west of Baldwyn. No! Don't y'all understand he's ours now? They left him." I ran to Ma, buried my face in her lap and began to cry. She always knew just how long to hold me close and tight.

Then, she dried my eyes with her apron and said in her gentle voice, "Linda Joy, Charlie is a Mooneyhan, not a Gholston. He belongs with his Mama and Daddy just like you belong with yours. I love you so much and if God wants you to have a little baby He will send you one. This is not the way to do it. Do you understand?"

"Yes ma'am, but Ma I really want me a brother or sister."

"I know you do. Now, run and bring me the apples Charlie picked. Y'all have all afternoon to play so don't mess it up crying."

"Ok, I love you Ma."

Out the door I went, and for the afternoon, my brother, Charlie and I played up a storm.

Daddy came home from the salebarn a happy man because he made $11.31 after paying Clovis his share and the auctioneer fee. It wasn't long until he saw Charlie. Daddy acted like Charlie and I were stuffed animals sitting on the couch. He said to Mama, "What's he doing here?"

She told him the whole story. Daddy stared right at me and said, "Girl, I ought to wear you out. I got to milk cows, eat supper and then take this boy out west of Baldwyn. You beat anything. You know it?"

"Yes sir" I said in my weakest voice, "I just wanted me a brother."

"If God sees fit to give us another child, I pray it's a boy. Two girls would drive me insane," Daddy said as he was half-way out the door to milk. After he finished we ate cornbread and milk for supper and in Uncle Bulich's borrowed truck we headed west of town. I was about to be an only child again.

We pulled into the yard of an old unpainted house that looked a lot like the Taylor House. It had a low front porch across the front and a dim, yellow porch light was on.

Mrs. Mooneyhan was on the porch. Daddy got out, picked Charlie up and walked to the porch. The windows of Uncle Bulich's truck were rolled down, so Mama and I could hear.

"Mrs. Mooneyhan, I brought Charlie home," Daddy offered.

"Mr. Doug, I knew he was safe with y'all. I don't know how we missed one of them young'uns; I thought we had them all."

Was Daddy going to say what I'd done? The few seconds of silence seemed really long to me.

"Well, could happen to any of us. Him and Linda Joy have had a big time. He's had his dinner and supper and Trixie washed him up some."

"Thank y'all. Sure enjoyed living on y'alls place. My husband said this evening we might be back with y'all by 'sprang'."

I whispered to Mama "How long is that?"

"How long is what?"

"Til 'sprang'."

"About six months."

Daddy was back in the truck, and our family of three went back to our home in Pratt.

Linda Gholston

Answered Prayer

After my failed attempt to create a brother for myself by scheming to keep Charlie Mooneyhan, I was once again alone. Larry McCarthy lived across the road, and we played together almost every day. Mama would make us picnics to eat in the yard. I always wanted mayonnaise on my biscuit and Larry wanted peanut butter. Mama was afraid he would choke on peanut butter and biscuit, so he usually settled for mustard and biscuit. Sometimes Mama would take us fishing in Duggar Creek, and one time she took us hunting! Larry had a BB gun, and it came a big snow. We got on our boots and coats and went rabbit hunting. I can't remember if we shot a rabbit or not.

I continued all of second and third grade wanting a baby more than anything. Playing at Ma and Pa's was fun, but I sure got lonesome. My cousins from Starkville, Robert Edd and Patricia, would come occasionally and we had a great time. Of course, at Ma and Big Daddy Butler's I played with Becky, but most of the time it was just me; and I wanted Mama to have a baby.

Christmas of 1955 I was in the third grade. Uncle Leroy told Becky and me that Santa Claus would park his reindeer at

Henderson Chevrolet before the Baldwyn Christmas parade. If we would be good he would make sure we got to talk to Santa! Wow! All we had ever done was stand on the street and see Santa come through town. Now we would have a chance to actually talk with him.

I wanted a desk for my room, some candy and fruit. Each year Mama would hang one of Daddy's socks on the mantle and Santa would fill it with fruit and a little candy. And, always under the tree would be one gift from Santa.

We went to Uncle Leroy's shop about an hour before the parade. Sure enough, sitting by the heater in Henderson's was Santa Claus. Becky and I were both a little shy, but with our mamas coaxing, we finally talked to him. He wasn't really friendly as best I remember but he listened. I told him I wanted a desk, candy and fruit. Then I whispered, "A baby."

He said, "Ok" he'd see what he could do. I'm sure he thought I meant a baby doll and that Mama had it covered.

On Christmas Day I got up and there in our little living room was a desk and in Daddy's sock was a coconut, an orange, an apple and some hard candy. I probably got some clothes although I don't remember.

There was no baby. I didn't mention to anybody that I didn't get the most prized gift I wanted. I honestly don't know if I knew the difference in Santa and God. I had asked Santa, so now I was going to really concentrate on asking God. Every night of my life I would say, "Please God, send us a baby of our own, not a Mooneyhan, but a Gholston."

Just before school was out Mama and Daddy told me they had a big surprise Mama was going to have a baby! Wow! "When?" I asked, hoping they would say "tomorrow."

Mama said, "Well, school is about to be out, and it will be summer. Then when you go back to school you will be in the fourth grade. You will be nine in October and the baby will come sometime around then."

Golly! All of that sounded so far away. I would be nine and get a baby in October. The statement, "slow as Christmas" took on a new meaning for me. Finally, summer was over, and school started. Then came September and finally October, and the only birthday party I ever had. Daddy saddled my horse "Go Boy" and all the kids rode. We ate cake and homemade ice-cream. This was October 6, 1956.

Several days later, Mama told me that I would spend the night with Ma and Pa as she and Daddy would go to the hospital early the next morning to get her. I don't really remember that night, but I'm sure none of us slept very much.

Pratt School had three class rooms and six grades. Grades one and two were in the classroom on the north and Mrs. Winnie Pratt was the teacher. On the South side were two classrooms. The one on the front of the building housed the third and fourth grades and just back of it was the classroom for the fifth and sixth grades. Aunt B taught third and fourth and served as principal and Mrs. Lillian Hopkins taught fifth and sixth. Only one phone was in the school, and it was in the lunch room.

Before noon, October 16, 1956 there was a knock at Aunt B's door. I was sitting on the fourth-grade side and Mrs. Ozell McCarthy, who ran the lunchroom, opened the door and let out her signature laugh. It was joyous and came deep from within. "Linda Joy has a baby brother," she announced.

I didn't move.

Aunt B asked, "Are Trixie and the baby ok?"

"Yes, both are just fine, Douglas said." She closed the door and we continued our arithmetic.

"God, thank you" I whispered.

Spiritual Note

As I recalled and wrote the two preceding stories, "My Brother, Charlie" and "Answered Prayer" I have reflected upon a great truth: When we pray a specific prayer to God we need to wait for God to answer. It becomes so easy for us to take on the role of 'Answerer of Prayer.' I wanted a brother or sister, and when I saw an opportunity to create one I jumped on a plan. I got Charlie for a few hours as a playmate but not really as a brother.

But when, on October 16, 1956, God answered the prayer it was perfect! Keylon Douglas came into our lives and changed them forever – for the good!

We have now enjoyed many years as brother/sister and I count him as a good friend. The blessings of my brother are too many to recount.

As you read these rambling accounts of my childhood I hope a take away is the indisputable value of prayer. Pray specific, bold prayers and record them and God's answers. You may be amazed at God's goodness and His desire to delight us.

When His answer is "No," rejoice that something better will be the answer.

When His answer is "Yes," rejoice and give testimony. When His answer is "wait," trust Him and wait.

Mama loved telling about her grandson, Cole's perception of prayer when he was five years old.

As she was getting him into bed one night she reminded him not to forget his prayers. He told her to go first. So, Mama began to pray for the family. When she called my name Cole asked, "Nannie why are you praying for Aunt Linda?"

"Because she's my daughter."

"Well," said Cole, "Don't pray for her. She has everything."

This story has been shared for about thirty years, as our prayer lives have evolved and grown. We mature from five years of age, seeing God as a big Santa Clause to maturity and realizing that Abba Father wants to bless us beyond measure. He owns the cattle on a thousand hills as well as the hills. This heavenly Father delights in blessing his children.

Cole, now with kids of his own, has a deep appreciation for God's goodness.

The Chiropractor

In the early 1960's Mama suffered from a "catch in her back." It was one of those things that just would not go away. She couldn't sleep at night; and it was beginning to affect every aspect of her life. Daddy took her to Dr. Gene Caldwell, and he used everything in his arsenal to help her. She would be better for a few days and then it would catch again. This went on for weeks.

Finally, Dr. Gene said to her, "I'm going to recommend you go to a chiropractor. I don't usually do that, but we're not making progress with your back. Dr. Stults has been practicing for years, and he certainly won't hurt you."

Mama agreed. Although she had never used a chiropractor she needed help. She and Daddy knew and liked Dr. Stults. I was in school with his kids. Dr. Stults was pastor of First Christian Church in Baldwyn and had a large chiropractic business.

One Saturday morning Daddy told me to watch Keylon; he was taking Mama to Dr. Stults. She had a bad night and was ready to try anything. The Stults lived on a high hill and from the sidewalk there were several steps to climb. Daddy got behind Mama and pushed.

I can only imagine the sight of those two getting up the steps. Finally inside, Dr. Stults said, "Trixie, Doug and I will help you on the table, so I can examine you." Mama said it took some time and she hollered a lot but finally she was positioned. Dr. Stults began to press until he located the exact pain and place of soreness. He had her roll onto her stomach and said, "Trixie, I'm going to do an overall alignment and then get that kink out that is causing your problem." Her first chiropractic adjustment, and she said she heard bones cracking and popping. Then he put his hand on one spot and said, "Bear with me."

Instant relief. Mama said no sooner than he released the pressure she felt the pain and tightness disappear. She was able to get herself off the table with no assistance. This is a woman who had been half bent over for weeks!

Daddy cleared his throat and said, "Doc, that's' the best I've seen her in ages. What do I owe you?"

"Two dollars. I work on the family plan. It's two dollars if I adjust one or twelve."

Mama said Dr. Stults had not gotten this out of his mouth, she turned around and Daddy was on the table. He always made the buffalo squeak on nickels; and he wasn't about to miss this bargain.

Dr. Stults said, "turn on your stomach."

Mama said Dr. Stults began at Daddy's waist and worked toward his neck. Every time Daddy popped Mama said he hollered, and that somethings he said were not appropriate for a preacher to hear.

When his adjustment was over she had to help him from the table. He paid. They left. They got to the steps and Daddy said, "That son of a gun has 'bout killed me. Help me down these steps. I'll never be caught here again if God will help me get to my truck."

Mama would tell this story and simply conclude with, "We got the family plan. He helped me up the steps and I helped him down."

Daddy would add, "Nearly caused me to lose a crop."

Linda Gholston

Healing

Ma Gholston and I saw Uncle Edd's car as it turned on to the long driveway that hot, sultry August afternoon. We'd had a brief thunderstorm about two hours earlier so the heat and humidity were intensified.

Ma and I were sitting on the front porch swing trying to keep the sweat mopped from our foreheads in great anticipation of the sight we now saw.

"Here they come, Ma!" I exclaimed as if she were blind.

"Yes, that's them. Thank you, Lord for safe travels. Run and tell your Pa," she offered.

Pa was in the front room with the fan and television, both set on 'high'. He liked to be cool and he was hard of hearing.

"Pa, Robert Edd and Patricia are here!" I was so excited.

"Well, did they drive themselves?"

"No Sir. Uncle Edd and Aunt Lorene are with them. Come on, Pa!"

By the time I was back to the front porch Uncle Edd, Aunt Lorene and Patricia were greeting Ma.

"Where's Robert Edd?" I asked.

At that very moment I saw him crawl out of the backseat of their car. His right leg had a bandage from just below the knee almost to the ankle.

I leaped off the porch and ran out to meet him. My partner in crime was injured.

"Robert Edd, what happened to you," I asked as I gazed at that thick bandage with a lot of tape.

"I gashed my leg yesterday and it sure hurts," he said.

We got to the porch. Robert Edd gave Ma a hug and then shook hands with Pa.

Both wanted a full account of Robert's injury. He said, "Let Mama and Daddy tell y'all. I got to lay down and prop this leg up."

With that he was opening the front screen door and hobbling inside. I got pillows and he propped his leg on the couch in the front room. I turned the fan directly on him and realized this was not going to be our usual visit.

By now, Aunt B, Uncle Bulich, Mama and Daddy had joined the other adults on the front porch. Patricia was pushing Keylon, in the red swing on the east end of the front porch. Although we couldn't hear clearly, Uncle Edd sounded like a judge holding court as he explained Robert's mishap.

"We almost stayed in Starkville," Uncle Edd said, "but Robert Edd said he would rather be here, so we just came on up. We have plenty of gauze and tape so hopefully he will be fairly comfortable."

On Friday nights we generally skated in the hallway. We only had one pair of skates, so Robert wore one and I wore one. I was fairly good on one skate but never great on two.

This Friday night and Saturday would be very different. Robert just guarded that cut leg and I sat close by in case he needed something.

With an injured child Ma Gholston said all rules were off as to the amount we could eat and drink. She had made her famous lemonade and was fixing hamburgers. This was my favorite Saturday night meal. When Robert and I were drinking our third glass of lemonade I was pretty proud of that cut leg. Of course, it wasn't my leg!

Sunday came and after dinner everybody went to the front yard. Even in the shade of the massive oak, it was still very hot. Pa produced two big water melons from his patch. He had them in the well house since Friday, so they were very cool in spite of the extreme heat.

Only a few minutes after we all got settled in chairs and swings Robert said, "This makes my leg hurt worse. Let's go inside and watch television."

"Ok with me," I answered, "but nothing 'cept preaching gonna be on channel 9. (Only channel we got!)

Robert occupied the same spot he had laid claim to all weekend – the couch with plenty of pillows and the fan blowing air directly on him.

"Would you get me a glass of water and turn the T.V. on?"

"Sure thing!"

I was off to the kitchen in a flash and actually found some lemonade left from the night before.

As the clock struck three, Robert on the couch and me in Pa's chair, the announcer said, "It's the healing service with Pastor Oral Roberts." We both listened closely as Oral Roberts preached. The camera spanned the audience and we could see hundreds, if not thousands of people attending.

After a few minutes Oral Roberts became still and almost whispered, "In one minute I am going to pray for scores of people who have come for healing."

Now, his eyes seemed to look right at us as he said, "If you at home want healing just bow and touch your T.V. screen. We will be back in one minute."

Just as I was enjoying another swig of lemonade Robert abruptly sat up, moved the pillows and said, "Come on, we are doing this!"

"Doing what?" I was totally puzzled.

"We are going to get healed. Then, my leg won't hurt anymore." He insisted.

"But I'm not hurt or sick," I protested.

"Well, think of something fast. It's almost time," Robert said as he positioned himself in front of the old console T.V.

"Nothing is wrong with me," I said emphatically.

"Get down here," Robert said as he pointed to the floor in front of the T.V. set. "Just pray for him to make you skinny."

I so loved Robert Edd. I hauled my fat self onto the floor and placed my hands beside his on the T.V. screen.

Oral Roberts now began the prayer. Robert and I were palming the screen of the T.V. with our eyes tightly closed.

After maintaining this uncomfortable position for what seemed like a long time, Oral Roberts shouted out, "BE HEALED!" In a hush he added, "You may open your eyes."

I looked at Robert. Robert looked at me.

I asked, "Is your leg healed?"

"No" and he added, "You're as fat as you ever were."

This experience did not diminish Robert's or my belief in prayer. To this day we both can say that God has heard and answered multiple prayers from both of us.

We have also learned that real prayer doesn't require holding on to a television screen.

Sitting Up with The Sick

As a child I remember often Mama going to "sit up," (as it was called) when people were very sick. This was the custom and all the neighbors would take turns "sitting up" at night which meant being there, assisting the patient and allowing the family some much needed rest. Some of the women were just too afraid of sickness or maybe death, but Mama always took her turn.

I remember going with her on a Sunday night to "sit up" with Mrs. Neely. I was probably eight. The Neely's lived in "the bend." The "bend" began by turning right at Mr. Boyce Norton's Store and making a horseshoe that ended at the Itawamba County line. The Neely's lived at the far corner of the curve in the horseshoe road.

I don't remember her diagnosis; but I would guess it was bone cancer. She was fragile, and her bones broke very easily. Mr. Neely was a broom maker. People came from far and wide to get a Neely broom. He had cut broom sticks and had one secured to each of Mrs. Neely's arms and legs. The memory of seeing her like that will forever be with me.

About eight o'clock Mama put me on a little couch in Mrs Neely's room and covered me with a blanket. I went to sleep thinking how smart and kind Mr. Neely was to devise a way to lessen his wife's pain.

Another neighbor came at six o'clock Monday morning and Daddy came to get Mama and me. I would spend the day with Ma Gholston and Mama would get some sleep.

Years later, Mama was going to take a turn sitting with Mrs. Evelyn Malone. It was quite a different scene from the Neely's. The Malones had eight kids, four girls and four boys. The boys were young, a couple of them, Jimmy and Danny, were about my age. Jack and Jerry were even younger. We got to their house in Guntown about an hour before Mama's shift was to begin. Mrs. Malone was very near the end of life. The house and yard were full of people. A family who was so loved by so many.

Evelyn was a beautiful woman; and when I saw her I could hardly believe my eyes. She was frail and looked so sick. I just couldn't understand those kids not having a mama.

Mama shoved me outside and all us kids played chase in the dark. Times of sadness can change in the twinkling of an eye when other children are present.

After a while Daddy came for me. I wanted to stay as I had at the Neely's, but Daddy said it was time for us to go home, that we would come back in the morning and get Mama.

I vividly recall the dark of the night and Daddy, Keylon, and I chugging along in Daddy's pick-up truck. As we traveled I became keenly aware that Mama wasn't with us and soon the Malone kids would not have their mama. It's the first time I remember realizing that something could happen to Mama or Daddy. I was twelve.

The next morning Daddy, Keylon (he was about four years old) and I went early and got Mama. She looked tired. She told Daddy, "It won't be long until Evelyn's gone."

I am so grateful that I had my parents for many more years. I had Daddy until I was fifty-nine and Mama until I was sixty. Losing parents is difficult at any age. My prayers, since their deaths, have been that I will live life in a way to honor them. They and my extended family taught me values, principles and guidelines that serve me well. Mama and Daddy weren't very educated but were very wise. They weren't wealthy but were rich in love and grace. They weren't accomplished as the world records accomplishments, but they were sure good at discipline, rewards and setting high standards.

Linda Gholston

Daddy's Down

Dark came early. It was the first week of January, and school was back in session after Christmas. Our little family had settled into a comfortable routine. Mama and Keylon, who was three, stayed home; I went to school and Daddy worked at Baldwyn Farmer's Co-op each day. He would get home about five-thirty and "tend to things" while I did homework. Then we would eat supper, get baths, and watch a little television before nine o'clock bedtime.

This particular day was routine. Keylon was in my lap reading a book when Daddy came home from work. He immediately began to put on quilted overalls over his work clothes. With a thick cap and gloves in hand, he said, "Going to tend to things. Be back directly."

Mama said, "Bulich came by and said to tell you he broke the ice on the ponds about four o'clock so you wouldn't have to after dark."

"Well, I sure 'preciate' that. I fed hay last night, so I'll just have to milk the cows and feed the hogs. See y'all in a few minutes and we'll eat supper."

Mama answered, "We're having salmon patties, hot biscuits and cream corn."

"Nothing suits me any better," Daddy said as he went out the door.

Mama began to make biscuits and fry salmon patties while Keylon and I continued to read.

About thirty or forty minutes passed and we heard a faint knock at the carport door.

Mama immediately said, "Nobody uses that door. Who could that be?"

A light, faint knock again and before Mama could open the door we heard Daddy say, "Help me. Help me."

Mama swung the door open and there was Daddy with his head, shoulders and arms pulled up on the top step and his feet on the ground.

"Douglas, what's the matter?" Mama screamed.

"I think I've been shot," Daddy answered.

"Shot? Where?"

"The back of my right leg. Never felt pain like this. Y'all help me in,"

Daddy's voice quivered as the severe pain and extreme cold weakened his voice.

Mama and I pulled and tugged. Finally, we got Daddy into the dining room, and Mama closed the door.

We helped him through the kitchen to their bedroom. He sat on the side of their bed and got his coveralls and pants off. No blood.

Keylon was crying uncontrollably and shouting, "My Daddy's shot! My Daddy's shot!"

While I tried to console him, Mama tried to touch the calf of Daddy's right leg, but he couldn't stand it. His pain was terrific although the leg appeared normal. Thank goodness, Mama gave him two aspirins.

Daddy slept very little and the next morning as I got ready for school, Uncle Bulich came to take Daddy to the doctor. We were all puzzled as to what was wrong. Daddy was seldom sick and never missed work. Today he did.

I was eager to get home from school to find out what was wrong with my Daddy. Mama saw me and opened the front door. A warm, glowing fire greeted me.

"Change clothes real fast Linda Joy, after you talk to your daddy for a minute. Me and you got to feed hay. Dr. Gene said "your Daddy's got a blood clot and will be on the bed for several weeks." By the time she was finished telling me the diagnosis I was down the short hall and into their bedroom. There was Daddy with his leg propped up on ice in an old rubber hot water bottle.

"Daddy, you ok?" I asked.

Keylon was on the bed playing so I had to give him a hug and play just a second.

"I will be. Just take time. Doc said a blood clot hit me. I'm to take an aspirin tablet every four hours and go back to him next week. Can't do nothing except get up to the bathroom and eat. Don't this beat the band?"

"Yes sir, it does."

Daddy added, "You and your Mama will have to take over 'tending to things' til I can get back on my feet."

"Me will help you Ninna," Keylon said enthusiastically. "Daddy, can Ninna not go to school? She gotta tend to things."

Daddy and I laughed a little.

"Get your barn clothes, Linda Joy. We got to go. Dark will catch us," Mama hollered from the living room as she added wood to the fire.

I changed quickly.

Mama put Keylon's cowboy boots on him, a big coat and a cap with flaps for his ears and snap under his chin. He fussed.

"Keylon Douglas, I can't have you sick. Now, leave that cap like I've got it. Hear me?" Mama demanded.

"Yes ma'am." He answered. Although he was barely three he knew when not to argue with Mama.

"I've already loaded the hay on the wagon while Keylon was asleep. I'll drive, and you cut the strings and throw the charges out." Then she added, "Get your Daddy's pocket knife."

At that time hay was baled in rectangular bales and tied with seagrass rope. When I cut the rope, the bale would immediately separate into "charges." (Smaller portion squares)

As Mama drove the little Ferguson tractor through the pasture all the cows came running because they knew hay was on the way! At just the right spot, Mama raised her right hand and I knew that was my signal to cut the seagrass strings and start throwing charges of hay, first one on the right side of the wagon and then one on the left. This procedure would continue until all the hay was out for the cows.

We had covered the upper part of the pasture and Mama pulled down into the lower pasture. I just continued to cut strings and sling out charges of hay to the right and then the left.

Suddenly, I realized the cows were no longer following us. They were in a circle and obviously mesmerized by something on the ground. A quick glance at the hay and I screamed, "Mama, stop the tractor!"

She slowly stopped. I was already out the back of the wagon. There in the midst of all those cows lay Keylon on his back with his boots pointed skyward. I grabbed him to my chest thinking he was sobbing. Very quickly I realized he was laughing… but not me. The cow poop and mud from him was now all over me.

"Ninna, I love'em cows. They just stood close to me and blowed hot air on my face. Felt good."

We were soon back on the wagon and headed home to check on Daddy.

For the next six weeks we fed hay every other day without incident. Daddy's leg healed and by Spring he was ready to plant the crop.

Anytime someone complained of being cold, Keylon would say, "Go let them cows blow on you!"

Ducks on a Pond

Somewhere along the way Mama learned to give shots. Today we might say "give an injection" but then they called it "giving shots." I think she first started when Ma Gholston was diagnosed with "high sugar" or diabetes. This was probably in the mid to late fifties.

Robert Edd ran through the house and threw a pecan. It struck and broke one lens in Ma Gholston's glasses. Uncle Edd whipped Robert. However, the entire family ended up thanking Robert. It was at an eye exam for her new glasses that her elevated sugar levels were found. She was immediately put on insulin.

Aunt B couldn't give Ma shots because she would faint at the sight of one drop of blood. So, Mama learned and helped Ma learn to self-inject. Back then, they used glass syringes that had to be sterilized after each use.

Mama would go anywhere in the community and give shots. This was a day when a license wasn't required, and neighbors were just grateful for the help.

I especially remember when Mr. Mink was very sick with lung cancer. He and his wife, "Hiss" had several school age children. As his pain worsened the doctor asked Hiss if anybody could give him morphine injections. He was in the hospital and so wanted to be home. That afternoon Hiss and two of her boys came to our house. She explained her dilemma to Mama. "I just can't do it, Trixie."

"Hiss, I'll be happy to come anytime; but one of the boys will have to run and get me."

"Thank you so much. Now he can have his dying wish – to be at home." Hiss said as she choked back tears.

The next day Mr. Mink came home. Mama took food as did many in the community. It became more and more frequent that their old black Chevrolet would pull into our drive and Mama would go to give Mr. Mink a shot. She would stay until his pain eased and then come home.

During his last days, I would often hear the horn honking at midnight or in the wee hours of the morning. The light in Mama and Daddy's bedroom would come on. Mama got dressed; and she slipped out the front door. We never locked doors back then.

One day the old car pulled in the drive, but the horn didn't honk. Hiss got out and simply said, "Trixie, he's gone." Mama held her, and they cried. Then she asked, "What do I owe you for all them shots you give him?"

"Why, you don't owe me one red cent. I was happy to do it." They cried some more.

Two days later we went to Mr. Mink's funeral. They wanted Mama to sit with the family. She did.

About a week later, the Mink's car pulled into the drive. Hiss and all the kids got out. The two older boys were carrying something about four feet long and three feet tall. They handed it to Mama and simply said, "We thank you so much."

The Minks had been to Fred's Dollar Store and bought Mama a picture. It was ducks taking flight from a pond. A very pastoral scene – one of serenity and peacefulness.

For many years that picture hung in the hallway of our house, ever a reminder of neighborly love and kindness.

Linda Gholston

Ma's Company

At age five my world was small, and my routine was consistent. Each morning after Daddy milked his cows and hauled the milk to the roadside he would come inside for breakfast. Mama made biscuits every day. We usually had eggs, some jelly or molasses with butter and in the summertime, sliced tomatoes and cantaloupes.

After breakfast Mama and Daddy would drop me off at Ma Gholston's and head to the fields. Ma would be finishing her breakfast dishes and starting dinner. She would work but we made a game out of everything. Often times I would ride my stick horse and chase bandits. She was the sheriff and I would come in and check on the bandits 'where a bouts' every few minutes. Then about ten o'clock she would sit in the front room and rest. We would get out the Sears and Roebuck catalog and play "wish." I would point to something I wanted, and she would say, "I wish this for Linda Joy." Then she would go into great detail describing the item. For a short time, it was like I had it!

Then she would choose an item and I would say, "I wish this for Ma." Same routine. I would describe, and her expressions would be those of joy and delight.

At five minutes til twelve she would have me ring the dinner bell that was right off the back porch. I would begin to pester her well before noon; but she stood her ground til five minutes before twelve. With each pull of the rope it would clang, clang, clang. Everybody in the fields would hear the call of the bell, come to the house, wash up and be eating by a quarter after twelve. About one o'clock they would head back to their chores.

Ma and I would watch "As the World Turns", then go sit out in the swing or maybe go to the garden. The afternoons were easy, fun filled. About five o'clock everybody would come in and go to the barns to milk cows, slop hogs and feed chickens, except for Ma's chickens. She and I fed them every day at four o'clock and gathered the eggs.

I can see Ma now with her bucket of chicken feed standing in the middle of the pen leaving the door wide open. She would distribute the food in a perfect circle about two feet on all sides of her. The hens and rooster would gather there and begin pecking at the food. I asked her why each time we went in for eggs she was careful to close the door but at four o'clock she left it open. She told me, "Because they have all they need." I have found great wisdom in that statement for years. When I was in college, a Bible professor said that heaven has pearly gates but no-where is there talk or reference to doors, locks or constraining fences. I thought immediately of Ma's wisdom. We will be with Christ and have all we need. Why would anyone want to leave?

So, each day was pretty much the same. Mama, Daddy and I would be in bed by eight o'clock, them up at four o'clock and me about six and to Ma's before seven.

One morning I remember getting there and finding things different. Ma was cheerful but seemed hurried. Her breakfast dishes were washed, dried and put away. Peas were shelled, apples and peaches in a basket and she was sweeping the floor. She never swept at this time of day.

"Ma, you ready to play sheriff?"

"Oh no, honey. I can't today. I've got too much to do. You run along now."

"But, Ma!"

"Linda Joy, today we are having company. Mrs. Stubbs is in Baldwyn and is coming here to eat dinner. Now, please don't bother me. I've got work to do."

"Yes, ma'am." I walked on the back porch feeling rejected and unwanted. Ma always had time for me. What in the world... I moped around for a while and thought I'd try again.

"Now Linda Joy, she's coming about eleven thirty. I want you to ring the bell a little early." What? We never did that. "And you offer her a glass of tea when she arrives." I thought Ma must have fever. Nobody drank tea except with their meal.

"Can we play "wish" now?

"No, I told you I'm very busy. Go to the orchard and help your Pa."

I meandered to the orchard and told Pa something was bad wrong with Ma, and that all she could talk about was Mrs. Stubbs coming to eat.

Pa laughed. "I'm proud she's coming!"

"You are?"

"Yes, it'll be like Sunday dinner, but it's only Wednesday." I headed back toward the house and sat on the front porch and felt sorry for myself. I saw a car turn in the drive. That must be Mrs. Stubbs. I ran in the house hollering, "She's here. She's here."

I couldn't believe my eyes! Ma had put on her Sunday dress! She had her pretty brooch on and her hair was neatly in a bun on top of her head held with a tortoise shell comb.

They embraced. "Oh Phronie, you are as beautiful as ever."

"Why Lillian, you haven't changed. How many years has it been? At least twenty, maybe twenty-five."

We got to the front porch and Ma invited her to sit in the swing while she checked things on the stove. She nodded to me and I asked, "Would you like a glass of tea?"

"Why, yes that would be lovely. What's your name?"

"Linda Joy."

I took the tea to her after Ma sent me back to ask if she used sugar.

"Yes, ma'am she wants sweet tea."

Doesn't everybody I thought, but didn't ask.

At eleven-thirty I rang the bell and the "earth stood still." Everybody came from the fields, washed up and greeted Mrs. Stubbs. We all got to the table and Pa "returned thanks." We never said, "ask the blessing" we always said, "return thanks." Pa said the exact same thing three times a day, 365 days a year.

"Father, thank you for this food we are about to partake of. Thank you for the hands that prepared it. May you bless it to our bodies and our bodies to thy service. Amen"

Was it ever a feast! Fried chicken, peas, butterbeans, corn, fried okra, creamed potatoes, beets, a pickle relish dish and sliced tomatoes. For dessert we had peach pie and apple cobbler. I don't know who enjoyed it more, Mrs. Stubbs, Pa or me!

After we finished I said, "Come on Ma it's time for 'As the World Turns.'"

"Not today, honey, Mrs. Stubbs and I are going to visit. Now you run and play." Insult to injury!

Pa went out under the shade tree to whittle and I went for a while. All he could talk about was how good that dinner was, and he hoped Mrs. Stubbs would come again real soon. Not me. About three o'clock Pa and I walked to Mr. Boyce's store and had our Coke Cola™. On the way home, I was just certain Mrs. Stubbs would be gone. No such luck.

"Pa how long will she stay?"

"Til sundown I suspect. They've got lots of catching up to do."

I wandered around in the yard pretending to be playing, but I was thinking. How could I get Mrs. Stubbs to leave? Nothing came. Then I thought, what would cause me to leave? A snake! I had a terrible fear of snakes. Just seeing one made me run like a jack rabbit. So, how could I get Mrs. Stubbs to think there was a snake in the house?

I rode my stick horse around back of the house. Pa's instructions were to keep me outside, but he was full of dinner, tired from walking to the store and too absorbed in his whittling.

I eased into the house and rather than going into the front room where Ma and Mrs. Stubbs were visiting, I went across the hall. This door was kept closed most of the time and reserved for spend the night company. It held a bed, a couch, and a chair, a piano and Ma's chifforobe, which had a large compartment on one side where she hung her dresses and pull out drawers on the other side. At the bottom of that side there was an opening for shoes. In that big wooden box was stored all the clothes my Ma Gholston owned. There were, at any given time, probably three to five dresses for everyday and one or two for church. There might be two or three pairs of shoes. One for the garden, one for church and one for every day.

I had a brilliant idea! I took a belt from one of Ma's everyday dresses and wound it like a coiled snake and for added emphasis, I pulled the buckle to stand up in the middle to look like it's head. This would do the trick. I strategically placed it in a dark corner by the chifforobe.

I looked at the coiled belt and lo and behold it looked so real. I started screaming "SNAKE! SNAKE! SNAKE!"

Ma came rushing out of the front room, "Where, where is a snake, Linda Joy?"

"Right there by the chifforobe, Ma. Everybody get out of the house."

"Let me borrow your stick horse" Ma said solemnly. She took my broom handle horse and raked the belt out of the corner. By now it had uncoiled and was obviously the belt to her black dress that had gray stripes.

Mrs. Stubbs was standing in the hall by now. Ma looked at her and said, "Sit back down, Lillian, and I'll getting us more tea. Linda mistook one of my belts for a snake. I declare, I kind of thought it was a snake at first myself."

Ma and Mrs. Stubbs drank tea and talked for another two hours. Later I heard her tell Mama and Daddy what I'd done. Never though did she embarrass me in front of Mrs. Stubbs by calling attention to "my trick."

The next morning, I got to Ma's before seven as usual. Before I could say anything, she gave me a big hug and said, "I'm ready to play sheriff, what about you!"

At Ma Gholston's all was right with the world.

Mrs. Gordon and Nancy

In the summer of 1961, Brother Laird from Laurel led the revival at Friendship Baptist Church. He talked about the small orphanage there and how the children were in need of host families at Christmas time. Even though we had very little, Mama and Daddy wanted Keylon (age 4) and me (age 13) to grow up with an appreciation for what we did have and a heart of generosity toward those who had less. So, they applied for a child. Several people in the church opened their hearts to these homeless children.

We found out in November that our child was an eight-year-old named Nancy. Uncle Leroy and Aunt Susie agreed to help buy her Christmas presents as did several other family members.

One cold December day Daddy left to go to the bus station in New Albany to get Nancy. About five o'clock Keylon, Mama, and I were waiting and saw the lights of Daddy's pick-up as he turned into the drive. They came in. Nancy looked ready to cry and Daddy held a paper sack with her few clothes. She wore only a little floral print cotton dress. Her only undergarment was panties.

"Where's her coat? It's freezing," Mama said.

"She don't have a coat. Let's eat and go to M. Gordon's. We'll have to buy her one, and she needs it now," Daddy answered. Keylon and I were showing her books and what few toys we had at that time. She mainly stood close to the fireplace and watched the flames.

We ate and headed to town. Mama and I went to M. Gordon's occasionally. One side of the store had clothes and shoes, the other side had appliances and furniture. Pa and others had told me "They are Jews" not being said disrespectfully but to show me a difference. I didn't know what a "Jew" was.

I asked Aunt B and she told me as best she could. She said, "They don't believe that Christ has come yet and they worship at a synagogue in Tupelo." Being so naive and hearing Baptist preachers all my life, I marveled that someone could believe that Christ had not been born in Bethlehem.

Though the Gordon's were as nice as could be I was always leery of them. Thinking Christ had not come was just beyond my comprehension. At school some kids made derogatory remarks toward the Gordons, but most people in and around Baldwyn seemed cordial to them. I don't know if they socialized with their neighbors or with other Jewish families from Tupelo.

We arrived at M. Gordon's before closing time. Being this near Christmas, they were open on Friday and Saturday night until eight o'clock. Daddy and Mama talked to Mrs. Gordon and told her that Nancy was from the orphanage and came without a coat. Daddy said, "We need something sturdy that will last her a couple of years."

"Certainly Mr. Gholston," Mrs. Gordon said.

As they chatted, Nancy had spied a lavender sweater with pearl buttons. She was mesmerized, rubbing the sweater gently as if it were cashmere.

Mama brought a car-coat over. It was brown and ugly but durable. Nancy eyed the sweater and asked in a whisper, "Could I get this?"

Daddy said, "Honey, that won't keep you warm. You got to have something to fight this bitter cold. Let's slip this one on." There stood little Nancy in the brown car coat slightly too large for her. Mama and Daddy talked about how the extra room would give her two good years of wear.

"Mrs. Gordon, we'll take this one. If you don't mind I'll pay you, and we'll just let her wear it. It's so cold and all." Daddy said.

"Yes sir, that's fine," Mrs. Gordon replied.

Mama glanced at a couple of things as we walked toward the door. A bell rang every time someone entered or left the store. Just as Daddy reached for the handle Mrs. Gordon from halfway back said, "Nancy."

We all turned as Mrs. Gordon walked toward us and handed Nancy a little white package with red and green ribbon. Mrs. Gordon smiled beautifully and simply said, "Merry Christmas."

After that I didn't understand anymore about being Jewish, but I sure loved Mrs. Gordon. She might believe differently but a little orphan had softened her heart as she did ours that Christmas.

Nancy looked beautiful in the lavender sweater with the little pearl buttons.

Measuring Head Circumference

Keylon was born October 16, 1956, the happiest day of my nine-year-old life. Also, born that day were Theresa Burcham, Jennifer Jones, and a little African American boy named Kokimo. The Burchams lived away, the Joneses were very wealthy, and Jennifer stayed in the room with her mom and a nurse most of the time. So, there for me to feast my eyes on were Keylon and Kokimo. A fine pair!

Mama had a C-section, so she and the baby stayed in the hospital for several days. Seemed like an eternity to me. He was doing well for the first six weeks of life, but then he got bronchitis. He was a very sick baby. Mama took him to the doctor. By then Daddy had bought a 1955 Ford pick-up so we no longer had to catch a ride or borrow a truck.

The next day Keylon was even sicker, so Dr. Gene Caldwell admitted him to the hospital. He was in an oxygen tent that had plastic sides secured under the mattress. My baby looked so little and fragile on that big bed with plastic enclosing him and a hose delivering oxygen. I prayed that God would keep him safe.

As quickly as he got sick, he got better. Generally, babies have a miraculous way of recovering much quicker than adults. When Keylon was about three months old, Daddy came home from the Baldwyn CO-OP where he worked, and told mama about a baby that was a month or so younger than Keylon. The family lived west of Baldwyn, and the baby had been diagnosed with "a water head." Now we know it was hydrocephaly, but then it was referred to as "water head" because water collected and enlarged the baby's head. I could tell that Mama and Daddy were very concerned about this baby and her parents.

Mama asked Daddy, "How did they find out?"

"I don't rightly know. Reckon her head is just really big," Daddy said as he began to eat supper.

Keylon was in a little bassinet sound asleep. I slipped in the living room where Mama had him by the fire and took a good look. At nine I didn't know that a baby's head is disproportionately larger than its body or that Gholston males tend to have large heads. I just stood there and looked at him after hearing the briefest, simplest definition of "water head." I was pretty sure he had it.

Mama said, "Come on to the table Linda Joy, and eat your supper. The baby's fine."

Daddy commented that it sure was unusual having to call me to the supper table. "How was school today?" he asked.

I told him it was ok, but my heart was breaking. I had to share with him and Mama that our baby had a "water head." I didn't eat much, and Mama checked my forehead. "No fever. Did you eat too much peanut butter and crackers when you got home?" She quizzed.

"Yes, ma'am I guess."

Daddy finished eating and went out to the barn to milk. Now days, he milked a couple of cows, just for our use. We had milk, buttermilk, butter and cream always.

"Mama, do you think Keylon has a water head?"

"Why no. He don't."

"How do you know?"

"I just know. Now help me get the dishes in the sink."

"Mama, I think he may."

"Linda Joy, don't be silly. That baby is perfectly normal. Now I don't want to hear that foolishness again. Do you hear me?"

Mama was not a patient woman with things that fell into the realm of foolishness in her estimation. The possibility that Keylon was hydrocephalic fell into that realm.

I did a little homework and went to bed worried about my baby's large head and how I would prove to Mama and Daddy that he needed help. It wasn't long until I had a plan. On the following Saturday I nonchalantly asked Mama if she had a tape measure. "No, I don't. Why do you need one?"

"Well, I was just looking at Aunt Maggie's the other day and wondered if we have one. Does Ma?"

Aunt Maggie was Ma Gholston's youngest sister. She and Uncle Hughey lived about three miles from us and she sewed for the public. Even when I was a teenager Aunt Maggie made my dresses. She charged three dollars to make a dress. Mama could buy the material, buttons and zipper for three dollars. So, Mama counted on six dollars to make a dress.

"Ma Butler has a tape measure I know."

"Yes, she does but don't go pilfering in her sewing machine drawers." Mama said.

"Yes ma'am."

"Can I go see Ma and Pa?'

It was a cold January Saturday. "Put on your coat, gloves, and a scarf around your ears." I had terrible ear aches as a child, still do occasionally.

So, I got bundled up and ran through the cotton patch to Ma's and Pa's house. Aunt B was grading papers, Ma and Pa were playing Dominos and Uncle Bulich was watching a western on

T.V. I watched with him. When the movie finished he said, "I better go tend to things before dark."

"Uncle Bulich, do you remember teaching me how to make a slip knot with that heavy string."

"Sure, I do. Do you remember how?"

"I think so. Do you have any string?"

"Yeah I got about half a spindle in the shop. How much do you need?"

I held my hands out to a length of sixteen to twenty inches I guess.

"Oh, I can spare that much. I'll stop at the shop and get it on my way back from the barn."

"Thank you, Uncle Bulich."

In about an hour he came in and got really close to the fire. He said, "Well, everything tended to again. I had to break the ice in that old drum them heifers drink from. That wind will chill you through and through."

He reached his hand into his pocket and pulled out a length of string, good sturdy, cotton weave string. "Will this do you?"

"Oh, yes sir! Thank you." I got on my coat, gloves and scarf and took off.

In my room I tied the slip knot and was ready. Daddy was feeding, and Mama went to the kitchen to start supper. She said, "You watch the baby." I had my "diagnostic tool," and was ready. As soon as I heard Mama clanging pots and pans I fitted my string snugly around Keylon's head. Not knowing the baseline circumference, this would serve as my starting point. I hated to break the news to Mama and Daddy, but after the evidence they would agree his head was way too big... a "water head" for sure.

The more I measured his head, the more I felt it needed measuring. There was little change over the weeks (slight but not significant). My measuring string was sure dirty. I tried marking it with Daddy's ink pen and made a real mess.

Occasionally, but not often, Mama would come into the room and catch me measuring Keylon's head. She kept telling me to stop, that it was silly and to put that string away. I would for a while. When Keylon was about seven months old he was tired of having his head measured. He could sit alone, and it was hard to hold him still and get the string around his head. If he only knew this was for his good.

One night a couple of months later, I was getting my measurement when Mama walked into the room. She was probably tired and maybe feeling bad, but she exploded. "Have I not told you time and again to stop putting that filthy string around that baby's head? What's wrong with you? Give me that string."

I didn't have to hand it; she snatched it, and it went into the fire. I watched as the string burned quickly and glowed only to die down almost instantly. I began to cry uncontrollably. Daddy came into the living room.

"What's wrong?" he asked.

Mama said, "I've never seen such a 'hard headed' youngin' in my life. She is determined to measure his head three or four times a day with a filthy piece of string. Tonight, it went into the fire."

One week later Keylon took his first steps. We were all so excited and thrilled.

"Daddy, can a baby with a water head walk?" I asked.

"No, I don't think so," Daddy said. "Maybe when they are two or three they may can. I don't know."

My measuring tool was gone and by September, Keylon was walking everywhere and beginning to talk. All thoughts of his "water head" disappeared from my mind and heart.

Linda Gholston

Earliest Remembrance

When I was about four months past my third birthday we had snow and ice. Mama said she had a roaring fire in the big fire place and had me dressed in layers. The bitter wind was blowing fiercely and caused the flames to dance high and low. The howling wind was making an especially lonesome sound about eleven o'clock that morning. Daddy was still milking cows, feeding hogs, adding extra hay and breaking ice on the ponds.

Mama heard someone banging on the front door of that little red house. She eased it open afraid of what the terrific wind might do to the fire. There stood Big Daddy Butler. He was dressed in his hunting clothes, with a heavy coat, knee boots, gloves and a hat.

"Daddy what are you doing out in this weather?" Mama asked. "Is somebody sick or dead?"

"No, everything good

I reckon. Just about to freeze to death. Are y'all ok?" he asked as he took his coat off.

"Yes, we're good. Douglas is tending to things. I cooked breakfast and made soup and then closed off the kitchen, so this room stays fairly warm. I've stuffed rags in the worst places in the floor," she said as she pointed to the stuffing.

"Well, your Mama and me was a talkin. We're afraid the baby will just be too cold, and I've come to get her. Truth is, your mama is afraid she'll freeze to death."

Mama said she laughed a bit. That was like Ma Butler. She always thought something bad was about to happen.

"Why Daddy, you know we are not going to let Linda Joy freeze. She is loving playing by this fire."

Mama had turned a couple of straight back chairs on their sides and placed them in front of the fireplace, so I would not get too close.

"Well, you know your mama as well as I do. I can't go back to Friendship without her."

Mama knew Big Daddy was in a pickle. After a while Daddy came in the house.

"Mr. Noel, weather's mighty bad. Are y'all ok?"

My Bundle of Early Life

"Yes, we're fine. Rosie thinks this youngin may freeze and sent me to get her."

Daddy laughed. "Tell her you found her outside with no shoes and nothing to eat." Without missing a beat, he added, "Trixie, you better bundle her up or Miss Rosie will be over here herself. Hate for her to try to walk over four miles on the ice."

So, Mama got a few clothes together and then bundled me up. She and Daddy got hugs and kisses and Daddy said to Big Daddy, "Tell Miss Rosie we'll be after her when it thaws some, and tell her I want some of her homemade tomato soup."

My earliest recollection is of sitting on Big's shoulders walking across the bottom. I don't remember leaving Mama and Daddy nor do I recall arriving at Ma Butler's. I just remember the sun glistening on the ice and the rhythm of the crunch as Big walked. I knew with him I was safe.

I am blessed that my earliest memory is one of safety and security. Having had some fearful, anxious times in life, it's so reassuring to know that our Heavenly Father holds us safely and securely even when life's weather is cold, turbulent or stormy.

One of my favorite passages of scripture is:

Psalm 57:1-2

Have mercy on me, O God, Have mercy!
I look to you for protection.
I will hide beneath the shadow of your wings until the

danger passes by.
I cry out to God Most High. To God who will fulfill his
 purpose for me.
                    (New Living Translation)

Teamwork

Over the years I have learned many valuable lessons regarding teamwork, perhaps none more valuable than the one Pa Gholston taught me about Jack and Sally. They were Pa's mules.

Every day Pa would work in his orchard plowing with Jack and Sally. Pa had those two mules for years before I was born. Jack was brown, and Sally was white with some black spots. This trio worked together six days a week, the mules in their harness and Pa following the plow.

At five minutes before twelve each day, Ma Gholston would instruct me to ring the dinner bell and immediately I would run as fast as my fat little legs would go toward the orchard. As soon as Pa heard the bell he headed Jack and Sally toward home. The further I could run the longer I would get to ride one of the mules. On this particular day Pa had just gotten his team of mules out of the orchard and onto the farm road when I raced up to him. He gave me a big hug and hoisted me onto Sally's back. The sky was blue, the wind was warm, and all was well.

As we moved slowly toward the house, Pa said, "Sister, I'm gonna have to get rid of one of these mules." Surely, I misunderstood. Sally and Jack were as much a part of the family as I was.

"What Pa?"

"Yeah. I just don't understand 'em. For years they have plowed together – been a real team of mules, but lately all they do is pull a part and we can't get nothing done."

I came off that mule's back and shimmied down her left front leg as fast as I could. I grabbed Pa by the britches leg. By now tears were flowing. "Pa, I love Jack and Sally. We have to keep them. Please."

"Sister, you only keep mules to plow, plant, and lay by the crops. When you got two, they are a pair. A team. 'Sum'um' has got into one or both of 'em, and they're not a team. They pull to the side, Jack to the left, Sally to the right, when I need 'em' to pull straight ahead."

I walked beside Pa the rest of the way to the house. He fed and watered the mules. He washed up and sat down at the table. I was still in shock.

As he ate his peas, corn, potatoes and corn bread he said, "When your Aunt B gets home from school what about a game of Dominos? Me and you will be partners, a team."

I sure hated to see Jack or Sally go, but I understood that Pa had chosen me for his team, and I'd better play best I could!

Some twenty years later I was trying as best I could to be a Sunday school teacher, teaching the ladies class at Friendship Baptist Church. I shall never forget how supportive those women were of someone who knew very little and had no experience teaching.

Mrs. Ressie Grissom, who really knew the Bible, and Mrs. Bessie Hopkins, who was almost totally deaf would sit each Sunday, smile and nod encouragement toward me. I shall forever love the memory of those two!

One Sunday the literature had a lesson on "team work." All week I kept thinking that these ladies will have no interest in a lesson on "team work." Little did I know that after our prayer requests and announcements Mrs. Earline Blassingame would be prepared to share with us the best example of teamwork I've ever heard. I've used this throughout my career in teaching on leadership and teambuilding.

Mrs. Earline graduated high school at Wheeler, MS in 1937. She said their graduation ceremony was scheduled for seven o'clock Saturday night. On Friday, the class sponsor told the class to meet her in the small auditorium at ten o'clock Saturday morning for rehearsal. Some boys said they needed to be in the fields, but she insisted on a short rehearsal of how to walk in, where to sit, when to stand, etc.

I believe Mrs. Earline said a total of fourteen graduated that year.

On Saturday morning the entire class showed up at ten o'clock. They practiced and were about to leave when the class sponsor said, "Oh, girls wear your best Sunday dresses and boys wear dark pants and a white shirt."

One boy hesitantly said, "Ma'am I don't have no dress pants. I got a white shirt, but all I got to wear with it is overalls."

The class was quiet. The sponsor said, "Ok if that's all you got just come in that."

Mrs. Earline closed with, "All fourteen of us left and walked to our farms. We had no way to talk to each other that afternoon… I got to the school about twenty minutes before seven in my Sunday dress and there stood all six boys who were graduating. All were in overalls with a white shirt. Now that's teamwork."

Aunt Tannis

For weeks I have agonized over writing about Aunt Tannis. I want to be respectful yet accurate as I recount what I was told, what I sensed, and what I experienced. If I had to use only one word to describe the life of my Aunt Tannis it would be: SAD.

She was born December 27, 1924, Ma Butler's and Big Daddy's oldest child. She was beautiful with an equally winsome personality. Little did she know as she grew up in the Friendship community that she would meet and fall in love with one of the Gholston boys from Pratt. Loving him brought her total fulfillment and great joy. Losing him brought her years of unresolved grief and great loneliness.

Uncle Marvin and Aunt Tannis were married November, 1942. To hear both my grandmothers tell it their courtship was sweet; both knew they were meant to be together. She saw him go off to war in 1943 and received news that he had been killed in June 1945.

Being a widow at twenty-one was a position in life she wasn't equipped to handle. Her choices on how to cope were not healthy. Ma and Big Daddy Butler seldom talked of Aunt Tannis' problem.

I'm sure they were dealing with her grief and astonished and disappointed at her reaction. Ma Butler said to me one day during a very brief conversation about Aunt Tannis, "Once your Uncle Marvin died, she just went wild, went berserk."

Very quickly she married Lawrence Roper. He was a neighbor who had never married. My sense is he loved her, but her capability to love deeply had been buried at Friendship cemetery. She and Lawrence struggled for several years. I remember going to see them as a little girl and sensing her sadness and his loneliness.

They had the only brick house in the family and Aunt Tannis got a new car most every year. Their house was surrounded by pecan trees and hay fields. I would play and watch Aunt Tannis light one cigarette from the butt end of another. There were ash trays all over their house, and at that time I didn't know she drank herself to sleep every night.

Often, she would hug me closely and say "Peek-a-boo, you're the closest thing I'll ever have to Marvin." Had I and others only known how to help her reach out for help. I guess none of us did at that time. We all loved Aunt Tannis and gave her sympathy and pity when she needed professional help and tough love.

Finally, Uncle Lawrence gave her an ultimatum. She either stopped drinking or she moved out. She wanted to stop drinking and would until the demons raged, and she would numb her broken heart once again with vodka. So sad.

They divorced, and she worked as a waitress at Mike's restaurant in Tupelo. Daddy, Mama and I went in one day at lunch. It was the nicest restaurant I had ever seen. She wasn't real busy, and Daddy said we could have a hamburger for dinner. She seemed to love us being there. I can see her now in that starched uniform. She introduced us to everybody. I remember thinking, "Aunt Tannis is famous. She knows all these folks from Tupelo." I didn't know one person from Tupelo.

While working at Mike's she met Richard Moffitt from Henderson, Tennessee. He was a traveling salesman who sold Kelly meat products and was smitten with her beauty. I remember him coming to Friendship to meet Ma and Big Daddy. Shortly thereafter they were married.

They lived at Pickwick for a few years. Both loved to fish, so this seemed fine with Aunt Tannis. She would come to visit, and we would all go to Ma's and Big's house. Never remember sensing any true happiness from Aunt Tannis while they lived at Pickwick.

Then they announced they were moving their house trailer and putting it in the woods very near Ma and Big Daddy. Both Ma and Big were thrilled! When the trailer arrived, it was not what any of us expected. Aunt Tannis and Uncle Richard were living the "Tiny

House" phenomenon long before it was fashionable. The little trailer had a tiny living/dining area, small kitchen, bath and bedroom that literally held a bed and one small night stand. I would guess the trailer was not more than 150 square feet. They did add a front living room and a small porch.

I remember getting to Ma Butler's one Sunday for lunch when I was probably fifteen or sixteen years old. Ma was crying. Mama hugged her, and Ma said, "Tannis is drinking again." Ma seemed totally defeated and exhausted. She was a proud woman, and to have a daughter who she loved dearly but couldn't understand seemed to be taking a toll.

She looked at me and called me Peek-a-boo. This was the nickname Aunt Tannis called me for as long as I could remember but not Ma Butler. She looked at me with the lenses of her glasses stained with tears and asked, "Peek-a-boo, will you go talk to her?"

"Yes, ma'am I will."

Out the door and down the drive I went. I didn't know what to say. She met me on the porch and began to cry. We sat there, and she said very little. I said even less. I don't know how much she had drunk, but she seemed pretty sober to me. She said that some days she just didn't feel that she could go on, that she died when Marvin died, and just a shell was left. I couldn't say that I understood because I didn't. I just hugged her and told her I loved her. She seemed lifeless, empty, without hope. How I wanted to make it all ok for my Aunt Tannis.

In April 1974, Aunt Tannis began to experience horrible headaches. I was in nursing school at the time and wondered if they were related to alcohol consumption. Soon she was hospitalized in Tupelo. They were treating her for migraines. When the Demerol wore off she would scream with pain. She kept saying that it felt as if a tight band was around her head and she couldn't stand it.

Finally, she was transferred to Baptist Hospital in Memphis. Richard and Aunt Susie followed the ambulance. They began tests and scans immediately.

Late in the afternoon on May 21st we received a call that she had a large aneurysm and must have surgery immediately. We got to Ma's and Big's as quickly as we could.

Daddy, Uncle LeRoy and I left about seven o'clock that night. Keylon was graduating high school so he and Mama stayed home. We got lost in Memphis but finally found the hospital and the intensive care waiting room. Aunt Susie was getting a nap, so we talked with Richard. The doctor had been out and told him there was a great chance she would be paralyzed and might not be able to speak. The doctor doubted she would know any of us. Grim situation.

The surgery began about six o'clock the next morning. At noon they were finished, and Aunt Tannis was in recovery. The doctor came to tell us that she had survived but only time would tell her condition. Every thirty minutes or so a nurse would give us a report saying her vital signs were stable.

About two o'clock Aunt Susie, Uncle LeRoy and Daddy left. They needed to get home and the rest of the family needed them to come home. It left just Richard and me. At about six o'clock that evening a nurse came out and said "Mrs. Moffitt is awake. She can have one visitor." I thought for sure that Uncle Richard would go but he started sobbing and said, "Peek, you go."

"Really? You want me to go?"

"Yes. Just come back and tell me the truth of how she is."

"Yes sir. I will."

The nurse took me back to a large critical care unit where beds were separated only by thin curtains on "U" shaped rods. She led me to Aunt Tannis's bed side. I took her hand and said, "Aunt Tannis, it's Peek-a-boo."

She gripped my hand and said, "Your Uncle Marvin was killed twenty-nine years ago today."

I stood there in shock. Could this be right? How did she know? She had been so sick for days could she possibly be right? I told her the surgery was successful and we just had to heal now.

As soon as I came home I went to Friendship cemetery and looked at Uncle Marvin's tombstone. He died May 22, 1945. Aunt Tannis had her brain surgery May 22, 1974.

She would live another twenty-one years and then go join her precious Marvin. I am grateful that Aunt Tannis seemed to enjoy life somewhat more after the recovery from surgery. Even on her best days one could sense incompleteness, a lack of wholeness.

Since 1945, she had a deep wound that would not heal. For a permanent heartache, she tried all kinds of temporary solutions – the numbing of alcohol, the arms of men she could not love, the smell of new leather in cars, fishing for ten hours when fish didn't bite and smoking three packs of cigarettes a day.

Had she had professional help, things might have been different. She spent a lot of time with various preachers and took many antidepressants. For as long as I knew her, a woman I loved dearly, lived on the perimeter and never in the center of life.

Aunt Tannis had an indescribable love for Uncle Marvin and he for her. Although it took years and caused much grief I think she learned that alcohol cannot return a blessing, nor can it heal a broken heart. She would be the first to say to those who will listen:

- Face your problems, and don't numb them.

- Pain must be felt and dealt with.

- God's grace is greater than all our sins.

- Heaven puts us in the presence of Christ and those who love Him and chose to be his followers on this earth.

Aunt Tannis will be at peace when I see her next. I look forward to that reunion!

Sayings

I grew up hearing a lot of sayings. I never gave the quotes or their pronouncements much thought until I realized how much these sayings influenced me.

Daddy told me hundreds of times, "waste not, want not." He also often said "a penny saved is a penny earned." He didn't believe in debt and would often quote scripture saying, "the borrower is slave to the lender." I learned from Daddy and others to live within my means. Somewhere early on someone advised, "give God ten percent of your earnings, save ten percent and enjoy the heck out of the remaining eighty per cent." All good, solid advice.

I can remember when cotton was up "a good stand" and we would hoe the grass and weeds. Daddy took an old hoe and cut the handle to about half its original length and sharpened the blade. Now, I could go with him, Mama, Uncle Bulich and others to the cotton patch. I felt so grown up and useful! Daddy or Mama would hoe behind me as I was not good, near the tender cotton plants. This was long before Round-Up, so the only enemy to the mighty Johnson grass was a well-filed hoe.

Often times, after a few minutes in the hot sun I would be thirsty and tired, ready to rest. Daddy would simply say, "Hoe to the end of the row." As a child I only applied this to literally hoeing grass from cotton. Now, I realize it applies to all of life. Your "cotton row" may be school, work, raising children, serving your church or volunteering in your community. Whatever it is, stick with it until the effort is finished. Daddy was a wise man full of good advice. Wish I remembered everything he taught me.

Mama was constantly saying, "When we get home you are getting a whipping." This sent shivers up and down my spine. I would always begin to beg and tell her I would do better. She would say "You had your chance, now you're getting a whipping." It might be hours before we would get home and I would be so very good. Thinking Mama had forgotten I would be breathing a sigh of relief, then I would see Mama coming with a switch. After the switching she would say, "This hurts me more than it hurts you." Somehow, I always doubted that!

Ma Gholston told me constantly, "If you can't say something good, don't say nothing at all." I haven't always heeded her advice but when I do, I find that I'm always thankful I didn't say what I was thinking. Hope I can heed her good advice for the remainder of my life.

Big Daddy loved to say, "You'll catch more flies with honey than with vinegar." What a gem of advice. Big was a well-liked man with a great personality. I don't remember him ever spewing vinegar. He loved pulling pranks and telling funny stories. He would pour some of his strong coffee in a saucer for me and add sugar. Sure, he would have used honey had he thought about it.

Ma Butler loved being at home, her main reason being she was afraid to go anywhere. If ever I knew anyone who thought the worse in every situation it was Ma Butler. Often times, I would watch her get dressed, pin her money in her bra, get her purse and announce. "Let's hurry up and go so we can get back." I find myself saying that sometimes.

When Uncle Bulich was speaking of someone who pretended to have more than they actually had he would gently say, "Big hat, no cattle." I love this saying and can't tell you how many times I have thought this!

Aunt B, being a teacher would often say, "Reading is the best, least expensive way to travel." She loved books and would often take me to the bookmobile, a big enclosed truck filled with books. We could check out three at each visit. Mrs. Bertie Patton drove the bookmobile. She was always smiling, laughing and filled with joy. She inspired all of us to read more.

Some days when it was raining and dreary Daddy would say, "The sky is always blue."

I would look up and see nothing but gray and black, and ask, "Are you sure Daddy?"

"Yes" he would say, "behind the clouds the sky is always blue." His favorite teacher, Mr. Lucian Agnew had taught him this. Throughout life I have often thought of this statement. No matter how gray, black, turbulent the clouds may be, the sky is always blue. What a wonderful truth!

These quotes, sayings, colloquialisms have served me well along with others I have learned. Another favorite is, "I drink daily from wells I did not dig." How true this is of the people in these stories from my childhood. They molded my principles, beliefs and theories of life. Obviously, hundreds of others have been added, but these are foundational.

Sign Language

I loved Mattie, Virgil and Jimmy Kimbrough. They, along with their parents, James and Ruby lived in the little red house. I was probably six or seven years old, the Kimbrough kids were all a few years older. To go from being the only kid on the place to being one of four was just grand to me.

Mattie, Virgil and Jimmy were all perfectly normal, very smart kids. James and Ruby were different though. They could not hear, nor could they speak. Today we refer to their condition as 'deaf mute' but in the 1950's they were referred to as 'deaf and dumb' by family, friends and everyone in the community. It wasn't a term of disrespect, but it certainly wasn't accurate either. James and Ruby were both very intelligent --- they just could not speak nor hear.

To communicate they used sign language. Of course, all three kids spoke English, but they also were masters at signing. They taught me, and I loved practicing with them.

November came, and we were ready for basketball season! Baldwyn and Wheeler both had good teams and we rarely missed a game. Most times, Mama and Daddy would sit with Mr. and Mrs.

Gideon Chism. The Chisms had lived "up north" for a few years and Mr. Gideon sounded like a "Yankee" when he talked. At least that's what Daddy said.

One night Baldwyn was thirty points ahead at half time and we were all a little bored. Mr. Gideon asked me, "What's new with you, Linda?"

"Well I learned some more sign language this week," and I began to show him different words and symbols. Daddy had gone to the concession stand. We got the same thing every game: 1bag of popcorn and two cokes. He, Mama and I shared. What I really wanted was a hotdog with mustard, my own coke and a moon pie. No money for anything extra.

After we finished our refreshments, Mr. Gideon wanted to see more demonstrations of sign language. I was happy to accommodate him, and we practiced most of the second half. With about five minutes left on the clock he asked Daddy, "Doug, y'all going to be at Wheeler Thursday night?"

"It'll depend on the weather. If I get things tended to in time we probably will. I believe they will go to State this year and I want to follow them as far as we can."

Mr. Gideon whispered to me, "You want a hotdog at Wheeler Thursday night?"

"Does ten pounds of flour make a big biscuit?" I thought. "Yes sir, I would love one!" Then reality struck. "But we'll just have popcorn and Coke I imagine."

"Don't tell your Mama and Daddy but I'm working on a plan. If it works you can have coke, popcorn, hotdog and moon pie." I was dumb founded. What plan could yield enough money for all of that? My stomach growled, and I could hardly wait for Thursday night at Wheeler.

We awoke that Thursday to rain. Daddy couldn't work in the fields. He told Mama he would pittle in the shop awhile after dinner and milk about four o'clock. This would give us ample time to be in Wheeler by seven o'clock.

Daddy bought our tickets and we walked into the gym about a quarter before seven. A good crowd was already there, and I saw Mr. Gideon waving and motioning for us. Daddy told Mama, "Yankee Chism is motioning for us to come sit with them." We made our way across the gym and sat with the Chisms. He motioned for me to sit by him. With Mama and Mrs. Chism between him and Daddy, in a hushed voice he shared the plan with me.

At halftime he told the others that he and I were going to the concession stand. Daddy could get his and Mama's refreshments, but Gideon would take care of mine. We left our seats just as the buzzer sounded and he went by the concession stand and picked up a Coke cup. They weren't plastic then, but rather a heavy paper with a paraffin coating. With cup in hand he proceeded to lead me to the opponent's side of the gym. "Don't say a word. Just do as I say, and, in a few minutes, you will have your hot dog." I loved hot dogs.

He got right in the middle of the game goers and in a very elevated, authoritative voice he said, "Ladies and gentlemen, may I have your attention." He clapped his hands a couple of times and the audience grew quiet.

"Ladies and gentlemen, I have with me a little girl who is deaf and dumb. She wants to sign for you." He nodded, and I put both hands in the air and began to share all the sign language I knew. "Can you help her with your spare change?" He asked as he began to pass the Coke cup.

People reached into their pockets and before long we had over a half cup of nickels, pennies and dimes and even three quarters.

"Thank you. Thank you very much" Gideon said and nodded to me and I signed, "Thank you."

In five minutes we were back to our seats with cokes, hot dogs, moon pies and popcorn. Of course, the money that wasn't spent went into Gideon's pocket. My Daddy couldn't believe it! He was amazed that Gideon had that much money. All he asked me was, "Did he offer to pay for that or did you ask for it?"

"No sir, I didn't ask."

"Well, ok then." Daddy said.

This plan worked perfectly until the last game of the regular season. Baldwyn played Wheeler. We were on the home (Baldwyn side) so at half time Gideon and I went to the Wheeler side. We got a nice amount of change and our usual supper. Wow! Was it ever good.

What Gideon didn't take into account was that a really good friend of Daddy's was sitting on the Wheeler side. The next week he exposed our scheme to Daddy.

Daddy came home and said, "Linda Joy, we need to talk."

"Yes Sir."

"Are you deaf and dumb?"

"No Sir."

"Do you know pretending to be in order to get money is dishonest? This really hurts me that you'd do something like this. I'll talk to Gideon and I don't want you to ever sit by him again. Do you understand me?"

"Yes Sir."

"From now on, you sit between me and your mama."

"Yes Sir."

I didn't hear the conversation between my Daddy and Gideon but there was never any mention of sign language again.

Wheeler made it to the north half finals. At half time Daddy, Mama and I had one bag of popcorn and two cokes. Daddy said, "Honesty is the best policy" as he handed me the popcorn to hold.

That popcorn and coke actually tasted better than the hot dogs and moon pies!

Dan For Christmas

Every farm girl needs a horse. For years I rode the little blue bike Daddy bought from Brownie, the peddler, for fifty cents when I was about five. In fact, for about a year I pretended the bike was my tractor. Daddy had given me a makeshift key and I would pretend to crank my bike. Problem was I would often lose my "key." Every time this happened my bike would sit idle. To my thinking, a tractor could not run without a key. Always within a few days or maybe a week I would discover my key and be on my way again. In my mind my blue, used bicycle was a gray Ferguson tractor.

The other ride I had was Sally's back. After Pa had to put Jack to pasture, he plowed with just one mule, Sally. Of course, this ride was only once a day from the orchard to the house. These two modes of transportation were sufficient, but I sure wanted my own horse.

One day, to my total surprise and delight, Daddy came home from the sale barn with an older Shetland pony. He was dark dapple gray with a light tail and mane. The most important fact was he was well trained and very gentle.

Daddy and Clovis Mink had been near Marietta buying some cattle to sell. As the farmer was getting them into the hallway of his barn, Go Boy ran in. The farmer said, "Doug, do you want that Shetland pony?"

"How much?" Daddy asked.

"Well, my boy has outgrown him. I got him a quarter horse over a year ago. Name is 'Go Boy'. He's getting older and some kid needs him. I'll let you have him for seven dollars since you bought these three heifers. Bet you can get ten at the sale barn."

Daddy just kept loading the heifers. He had figured their weight and how much he thought they would bring at the sale barn. The total he owed the farmer for the three was $77.50. He got out his billfold and said, "I'll load that pony and make it $84.00 if that suits you."

"Well, I'll throw in the saddle and bridle for two dollars. I ain't got no use for it," the farmer replied.

"Ok. $86.00 it is," Daddy said as he counted out the money.

Daddy and Clovis went on to the sale barn but didn't unload Go Boy. He was coming to Gholston Farms!

Go Boy and I rode many miles. He was slow but steady. I sure did love that little horse. After about three years Go Boy and I had a problem. I grew; he didn't. Finally, my feet were almost touching the ground and his back was swaying.

Daddy found me a bigger horse named Traveler. He was black with white spots, really a beautiful animal but not well trained. Daddy would lead me on him but didn't trust him for me to ride outside the pasture. That wasn't great fun. Uncle LeRoy told Daddy to wait until Sunday afternoon and he would come over and "break" the horse. (That meant train him.)

On Sunday afternoon Uncle LeRoy came and Daddy saddled Traveler. Uncle LeRoy got on him and began to ride slowly around the farm. Then he took him down the drive and turned to the left, headed toward Baldwyn. Suddenly, we saw Traveler start to snort and buck and Uncle LeRoy was flying in the air but holding on to the saddle horn. In a flash they were crossing Dugger Bridge with Daddy running behind them.

About twenty minutes later we saw Daddy and Uncle LeRoy walking and Traveler being led behind them. As they turned into the drive, Uncle LeRoy simply said, "That horse is wild." How right he was.

That year for Christmas Santa brought my cousin Becky and me 26-inch bikes, so I had a mode of transportation and seldom rode Traveler even in the pasture.

About three Christmases later when I was fourteen, Mama and I went to town (Baldwyn) on Christmas Eve for her to finish Christmas shopping. Keylon stayed with Aunt B and Ma Gholston because it was bitter cold.

On Christmas Eve night we all went to Lois and Curtis Glenn's for the Butler Christmas. Lois had baked a big ham for sandwiches and made chicken and dressing with all the trimmings. The real feast of the night would be the desserts she and Mama had been working on for what seemed like weeks. At least three weeks before Christmas they had "baking day" where they made fruit cakes. These were delicious. Lois would send Curtis to the liquor store for a pint of whiskey. After she and Mama baked three fruit cakes, they would let them completely cool. Having used tube pans they would place white cloth in the center of the cake and then saturate the cloth with whiskey. Each cake would be carefully wrapped in cloth, so no air could touch. They would be placed on Lois' dining table and every other day she and Mama would carefully remove the wrapping and pull the "whiskey cloth" so gingerly from the center.

After much sniffing and discussing they would decide on the amount of whiskey to add. After the cloth was sufficiently saturated, it went back into the center and all of the wrapping was replaced. For three cakes, this process seemed to take well over an hour. Lois would threaten Keylon, myself and any other kids around, should we even think about pinching a cake. We wanted to but knew better.

Several days later they would bake fresh coconut cakes, pineapple cakes and a variety of pies. Needless to say, as Mama and I shopped that afternoon my thoughts were on getting to Curtis and Lois Glenn's for supper. The adults had drawn names for the gift exchange earlier. Mama got Big Daddy's name and Daddy got Uncle LeRoy's. They drew the names on Thanksgiving Day, so why we waited so late to shop for these gifts I'm not sure.

We went to Gladys Barber's store and Mama got each of them a flannel shirt, perfect for this frigid cold weather. After Mama got a few other things we went by Howard Hopkins' Grocery Store and then walked to the CO-OP to wait for Daddy to close at five and then head home. We would get Keylon, then get ready to take our gifts and head to the Glenn's. It was about four o'clock when we arrived at the CO-OP. The heat felt so good and before long we were warm through and through.

Daddy had a small barn and feed lot next to the Co-op. He had bought thirteen tiny ponies in the fall and "Santa" had bought all of them for various children throughout the area. Ten had been picked up, but three that would be delivered to kids in town were still there.

"Come and go with me to feed the ponies," Daddy said.

Mama immediately objected, "No Douglas. You know she don't need to go out there." I thought she was referring to the cold weather.

"Oh, it won't hurt," Daddy insisted. "Tomorrow is Christmas."

Mama looked at him disgustedly and said, "We have a five-year-old at home, you know."

"It'll be alright," Daddy assured her.

I bundled up in my coat, gloves and scarf and out the door Daddy and I went. Thought I'd be napping on a feed sack, but here I was in a terrific wind helping Daddy feed the three remaining tiny ponies.

"Go in the barn and bring me a bucket of sweet feed."

"Yes Sir."

I walked out and held the feed close to me for fear it would blow out of the bucket. He took it and spread it in their feeding trough. "Let's step in here out of this wind," Daddy said.

So, into the rather dark barn we went. We just kinda stood there. Mama always said Daddy and I were the two most nonobservant people she knew. What she said was, "If it was a snake it would bite ya'll."

"You see anything?" Daddy asked.

"No Sir. Do you?"

"Look in that stall behind you."

I turned to see a majestic deep red saddle horse with a white blaze. I didn't understand.

"Wow! That horse is beautiful," I exclaimed.

"Whose is it, Daddy?"

"Yours."

"Mine?"

"Yes, Santa dropped him off here, but he'll be at the house in the morning. Do you like him?"

"I love him!! What's his name?"

"Dan. He's a fine saddle horse. Gaited. Will be a lot of fun to ride and he's broke."

"This is my horse?"

"Yes, but don't tell Keylon, he might be confused about Santa having him here. Ok?"

"Yes, Sir. Ok"

I rubbed on Dan a little and he nudged my hand for sweet feed. I was in total shock!

"We better get back to the store," Daddy said as he poured Dan feed into a bucket and checked his water.

We walked in total silence. Daddy opened the door, we walked in and he began to close out the register for the day. Without really looking Mama in the eye, he said, "Darnest thing, she found that horse."

Mama said, "Who does that surprise?"

Linda Gholston

Christmas Day

Normally, a five-year-old would be awake before a fourteen-year-old on Christmas. But knowing I was getting Dan I'm not sure I ever went to sleep. Our house only had two bedrooms so Keylon and I shared a room. I heard Daddy moving around, and I started gently poking Keylon.

The back door closed after Daddy started a fire in the fireplace, so I knew he had gone to get Dan. I lay very still. Then I heard Mama in the kitchen. She would be making biscuits, frying ham and cooking eggs. Usually, I would be excited about breakfast but today the thought of Dan took my appetite.

An 'eternity' later I heard Daddy open the front door, "Biggest snow we've had in years. About seven to eight inches would be my guess," he said.

Mama said, "I'm glad Edd and Lorene came yesterday from Starkville. At least everybody will be together at your mama's for dinner."

I began to poke a little harder on Keylon. He moved slightly and pulled the cover over his head. I dug down to his ear and whispered, "Santa Claus has been here."

With that he sprang up and said, "Let's go see!"

Mama had plugged in the Christmas lights and under the tree was a baseball bat and Sun Up shaving lotion, the two things Keylon asked for. Also, he had some clothes and another toy or two.

For me, there was a note (in a familiar hand writing) that simply said, "Go look in the trailer." We all got on shoes, coats and gloves. Keylon was mesmerized by the snow. It may have been his first snow, it certainly was his biggest. I ran and there was Dan! "Look, Keylon, look!" He was as excited as I was!

Daddy said, "Here's the bad thing. We can't risk him getting a leg in a hole. You can't ride in this snow. Let's get him to the barn after breakfast."

"When can I ride?"

"When the snow is gone, and the horse can see where he's going."

After we ate and Keylon played a bit with his toys, we took Dan to the barn and fed him. At least I could pet him, and Daddy let me sit on him in the hallway of the barn. That snow lasted almost a week. I spent a lot of that time in the barn.

All through high school I rode Dan. Wonderful memories!

Uncle Bulich

Sometimes I watch "Mountain Men" on television. I always think of Uncle Bulich. He was a big, tall man. Ma Gholston always said, "Bulich is strong as an ox, agile as a tiger, quiet as a mouse and gentle as a lamb." That sums him up pretty well. We all loved and admired Uncle Bulich.

In fact, Keylon and Teresa named their first son after Uncle Bulich – he was Samuel Bulich and Brent is Samuel Brent. Although Brent is named for him, it is Clay who most reminds me of Uncle Bulich. Clay has his stature, his personality and his good nature. I watch Clay working on the farm and it's like seeing Uncle Bulich fifty to sixty years ago.

Uncle Bulich was born March 11, 1921 and died on November 13, 1980. He was only fifty-nine years old. To give a glimpse into his stoic nature, courage and strong will; he was diagnosed with lung cancer one day and died the next. The doctor who tried to look into Uncle Bulich's lungs with a bronchoscope came out of surgery and told me, "I can't even get the scope to his lungs. I have never seen this before." Also, his great grit and love for food lasted until the end. I helped him sit on the side of his bed early morning on November 13 and he actually ate most of his breakfast. Unbelievable!

About one o'clock that afternoon he turned on his side and placed his left arm under his head just like he slept every night. I felt the end was near. Mama, Daddy, Aunt B, Uncle Edd, Uncle LeRoy and Aunt Susie were all outside the room surrounded by neighbors and friends. Keylon and Teresa had come from Aberdeen. Uncle Bulich looked up into the air and said, "Mama". I think Jesus brought Ma Gholston with Him to usher her second boy into heaven.

We continue, to this day, to tell "Uncle Bulich" stories. There are so many, but my favorite was the summer of 1952 just before my fifth birthday. Uncle Bulich and I had a Sunday afternoon ritual. We would check the cows and sometimes fish in the pond, but about three or four o'clock we would get in his mint green Chevrolet pick-up and go to Baldwyn to get milkshakes. We both loved chocolate milkshakes! Unless one of us was sick or Mama and Daddy decided to stay at Ma's and Big's for supper, you could mark your calendar that Uncle Bulich and I were going to get milkshakes – one each, we never thought of sharing one!

One Sunday afternoon he asked me if I wanted to go with him to check his cattle. Of course, I did!

We walked all through his herd and then he sat down on the hillside and I played around for some time. Finally, I went over and said, "Uncle Bulich, you 'bout' ready to go get our milkshakes?"

"Hon, I'm not feeling too good today. Believe we'll skip."

What? Skip a milkshake on a Sunday afternoon. Not me. Thinking it was a joke I said, "Uncle Bulich, we always go."

"I know, but I'm tired and feel bad. Think I'm catching a bad cold. You just play now and let me rest."

"Yes, sir."

Never was that going to work. I played around, and he sat quietly for probably another ten or fifteen minutes. Being an only child, I knew every adult in the family and how to pull their "chains". I was about to pull his.

I eased up behind Uncle Bulich, threw my arms around his neck and said, "You know Uncle Bulich, you just love me too much." Within fifteen minutes I was standing in the seat beside him in that old Chevy and we were headed to Baldwyn for two chocolate milkshakes.

Uncle Bulich had several different jobs, in addition to working on the farm. The first job he had that I can remember was hauling milk. He would leave at three o'clock in the morning and go to several farms, load the milk and deliver it to the processing plant in Booneville. He was usually home by noon and had the afternoon to plow, plant and harvest crops.

One time when Robert and I were nine or ten, Uncle Bulich said we could make the milk route with him. Goodness! We were so excited we couldn't sleep. He came into the east room at Ma and Pa's house about two-thirty in the morning to wake us. We were already up and dressed!

We rode in the dark from one farm to the other as Uncle Bulich loaded milk can after milk can. As the sun begin to break morning, Robert Edd and I fell sound asleep. About seven Uncle Bulich woke us. We were in Boonville and he was ready for breakfast. We feasted on fried eggs, biscuits and country ham.

After we finished at the processing plant, we back tracked and left each farmer his milk cans. They would be filled once more and at three the next morning, Uncle Bulich would start the process over again.

For many years Uncle Bulich worked with Daddy at the Baldwyn Farmers CO-OP. He drove the gas truck and kept all of the farmers supplied with gas.

Prior to this, I remember him working for a brief time as a short order cook. He taught me two things from this experience:

1). If you want hungry people to buy your food, just fry some onions on the grill top. (Sure works for me!)

2). If you want to tip the dish washer, order a glass of milk and leave a bit in the glass. Drop some change in the milk.

Uncle Bulich was a wonderful cook. His specialty for us was "pea sausage." He would take Ma's left over black-eyed peas, drain the liquid and mash them well. Then he would stir in an egg, salt, pepper and sage along with red pepper flakes. He then formed these into patties and floured them. When his oil (lard) was hot, he would fry them up! Goodness, "pea sausage" in a biscuit with some homemade jelly or molasses was hard to beat!

Uncle Bulich was a gentle giant who loved his family furiously, stood for right and was a perfect gentleman. He was a great role model for those of us who were fortunate enough to love and live with our Uncle Bulich.

As I mentioned, Brent is named in honor of Uncle Bulich, However, Brent looks and acts so much like my daddy, his name should be 'Little Doug'. Like Daddy, Brent has a sixth sense about buying and selling. Just as Daddy would buy cattle and make a profit at the salebarn, Brent can do the same with ATV's, dogs, tents, and Vespas.

One day I saw a silver Vespa in Brent's garage and asked, "Are you going to ride this?"

"No ma'am, I plan to sell it."

"Well Son, I am afraid you'll lose money. Those things are not very popular in our neck of the woods."

"Oh, I reckon somebody will want it," he chuckled.

"You sound like your granddaddy," I told him.

Two weeks later an attorney drove from New Orleans and bought the Vespa. Brent grinned and said, "Ain't telling you how much I made, but Granddaddy would be proud of me!"

Stay with Me

In the 1950s, Baldwyn was a trading center for the entire region. There were no 'big box stores' or malls. Everybody shopped with local merchants. Baldwyn was a bustling town especially around Christmas time. The merchants pooled their money for the "Saturday afternoon drawings." On the four Saturdays preceding Christmas, cash was given to the lucky winners.

Every time someone spent a dollar, he or she was given a ticket. The ticket holder kept the stub and put their ticket into a large barrel in the center of town each Saturday. At two o'clock the drawing was held. The first Saturday they drew four tickets and each stub holder got $25.00. Lois Glenn won $25.00 in 1953! We were all super excited! I had turned six in October and was in first grade. I knew $25.00 was a lot of money!

On the fourth and final Saturday, three tickets would be drawn. The first ticket was for $100.00, the second for $250.00 and the third ticket would award the stub holder $500.00! Can you imagine!

Mama explained to me that we were going to shop a little and stay for the drawing. In four weeks she had accumulated twenty-seven tickets from grocery and Christmas shopping. There must have been thousands of tickets in that big barrel!

The crowd was unbelievable. I had never seen so many people and thought it must be the 'population of half the earth'. People came from Booneville, Biggersville, Wheeler, Saltillo, Bethany and lots of small farm communities, like Pratt and Friendship.

As we slowly maneuvered, Mama would say "Stay with me." Sometimes I would lag behind looking at something in a store window and she would impatiently say, "Linda Joy, stay with me. You'll get lost."

Figure 1 anonymous / **This old picture depicts the crowds gathered for the Saturday afternoon drawing.**

It wouldn't be long until I'd get a couple of feet in front of her and she would say, "Linda Joy, I'm not telling you again, stay with me." The huddled masses were everywhere. Christmas was less than a week away and I'm sure that everyone there had visions of winning the five hundred dollars!

Mama slowly turned off the sidewalk on Main Street and headed down the steep incline on Second Street. It seemed to me to be even more people. Some were headed up hill toward the center of town and some in the opposite direction. It was hard to keep one's footing.

We walked about fifteen yards and I was being tussled about like a Teddy bear. Reaching and gripping Mama's hand, I looked up to see that I had the hand of a rather large, no nonsense appearing black lady. It was a different time then, and we were both afraid of the implication. She withdrew her hand as fast as I did mine.

From seven to seventy (and beyond) I've learned a lot about race relations in Mississippi. My family, as most of our kin and neighbors, believed and practiced, "separate but equal." It didn't take me long to realize that as a society the "equal" wasn't there. What totally reshaped my heart about people of all colors, races, and nationalities is salvation. I realized that Christ shed His blood for all people throughout the ages. Today I enjoy the friendship and fellowship of many who look different from me. Don't be afraid to learn from those who think, look or believe differently from you.

Not holding any hand, I searched through the crowd for Mama. I saw overalls, black coats, long dresses, corduroy pants – a whole assortment of dress. Mama's winter coat was a camel color and finally I saw it. I pushed with all my might and grabbed her hand with Samson like strength.

"Now, do you understand what I mean by stay with me?"

"Yes, ma'am." Mama didn't have to worry about my lagging behind or running ahead the rest of the day.

Often, when I read chapter five of Mark's gospel I am reminded of Mama saying, "Stay with me."

In this account Mark records rather vividly, regarding the man who lived among the tombs and the hills. Chains could not hold him; he was antisocial to the point of having to live on the perimeter rather than the center of society. He cut himself and wore no clothes. Fairly easy to imagine a visual image. An insane individual who froths at the mouth, is filthy and unkept, hair is long and stringy. Children feared him, and adults avoided him.

Then Mark says he sees Jesus getting out of the boat and recognizes Him as God's Son. The demons inside the man begin to beg not to be cast out of the country. (They sense His power) So, Christ casts them into a herd of approximately 2,000 hogs that are nearby. The swine begin to run uncontrollably and go off a cliff into the water and drown.

Those who were in charge of the hogs go with haste to report the happenings to the villagers and those who live round about in the countryside. They come, in mass, and see the healed man fully clothed and sitting as sane as any of them. They also see the drowned swine.

Their reaction is not one of delight, but rather one of fear. If the Christ has this power what could he do to them, their families, their homes, their businesses? Immediately they strongly encourage Christ to leave as is. As He goes to the boat, the man who has experienced the Savior's healing finally speaks. He simply asks, "May I go with you?"

In all of my years since I first identified with Christ I have done just as I did with Mama that Saturday. I have, at times, lagged and at times I have run ahead. The sweetest fellowship is when I walk and stay with Him.

Linda Gholston

How Many Cows

For the first five grades I went to school at Pratt. Never dreamed I would go anywhere else until I finished sixth grade. All of us, teachers, students, and cooks lived in the Pratt Community. We wore shoes to school but during the summer we were barefoot; riding bikes, helping with gardens and crops. Life didn't get any better!

Mrs. Lillian Hopkins was my fifth-grade teacher. How I loved her! Each Friday she would bring her accordion and play after our last recess until the final bell. I was mesmerized by her ability to play and sing. On the opposite side of the room was the sixth grade and I assumed I would sit there the next year and Mrs. Lillian would continue to teach us and play her accordion. Wrong.

During Christmas break I overheard Aunt B telling Mama and Daddy that Pratt would close at the end of the school year which meant I would start sixth grade in Baldwyn. This news ruined my holiday. Aunt B made the rounds to tell the news to all the parents she could. Supposedly, "consolidation" was the way to go.

In May of 1958, Pratt School officially closed. We all dreaded getting on the school bus in September and going into the big city of Baldwyn. A large crowd was gathered that first day. All of us from Pratt wore our best clothes and hoped to make a good first impression. Ma, Pa, Mama, Daddy, and Aunt B kept assuring me that everything was going to be ok. In fact, B had been my teacher for third and fourth grades and would end up teaching me sixth and seventh grades at Baldwyn.

Some of the town kids called us "country" but most were nice and accepting. We all doubted we were as smart as they were, but I reckon we held our own. Still, to this day I remember when Aunt B called on one of the girls to read aloud. B was a big believer in students standing, projecting their voice and reading. This girl was very shy, and B had her start over three times until people in the back of the room could hear her. She was reading about Hindu customs and said, "They worshipped 'scared' cows" instead of "They worshipped sacred cows" - everybody went hysterical. After that, the joke was, "Ya'll country kids go milk your 'scared' cows!" We were typical sixth graders!

Another student who wasn't accustomed to reading aloud came to the word Japanese and pronounced it "Ja-Panies". That brought on laughter again. However, many in this class would become life-long friends and we continue to enjoy friendships that span several decades.

In March of 1959, I was excited about school being out for the summer and actually looked forward to the seventh grade. Daddy told me we needed to choose the heifer I would show at the Lee

County Fair and Dairy Show in September. We decided on one and Daddy gave me a halter and lead to use.

I found a lot to do that summer and very little time to lead that heifer around. It was hot, and the flies were bad at the barn. Time was marching on!

Mama had gotten Aunt Maggie Mabry to make me three new dresses. I had two from last year that she let the hem out of and Mama said I could wear them 'til Christmas. Five days of school each week and five dresses.

I got serious about working with my heifer a short time before school was to begin. Each day I would put the halter on her, lead her around in the horse lot and brush her. She was looking good. Daddy enjoyed me showing the animals more than I did.

Saturday morning, I had my heifer haltered and ready to practice. School would start on Monday and I was ready. About eleven o'clock she was drinking from a bucket of fresh water and I was brushing her. I guess my right foot touched the bucket and she moved quickly. Her front left foot landed squarely on my big toe and I felt her twist. Oh, my goodness! It hurt so bad. I was barefoot of course, so I got the halter off of her and hobbled to the house.

Keylon was watching cartoons and Mama was cooking dinner. I called for her to "come quick"! She ran to the door and I sobbed, "My toe. That heifer broke my toe."

Mama got me inside and ran a dish pan full of water. I guess she added alcohol. I'm not sure. "Put your foot in here."

Blood and mud soon created a red tinged murky bath. Keylon started crying, "My Ninna (he couldn't pronounce L's) is hurt." Mama got his attention back on the TV.

She sat on a little ottoman and said, "Put your foot in my lap," after it had soaked for several minutes.

I didn't really want to, but I knew Mama meant business. She examined my toe closely and pronounced "That's nasty. You'll lose that nail. Gonna' be sore for a long time. Stay away from the barn and chicken pen."

She found a little gauze and tape. After saturating it with alcohol she applied the bandage. "When your Daddy gets here y'all go to Houston's Drug Store and get gauze, tape and mercurochrome. Linda Joy, I hate this, but you can't show that heifer. I'll wash all your white socks. You can't wear a shoe for several days."

"But Mama, school starts Monday."

"I know that, but you'll be going with two socks on that foot. Better not get it stepped on. You are liable to faint," Mama added.

My thought was I'll faint when people find out a cow stepped on me. Oh mercy. How embarrassed can a country kid be on the first day of seventh grade. I was about to find out.

Daddy came in, heard the story and we headed to Baldwyn. "Sorry about your foot. Believe you'd of placed with that heifer but there's always next year. You go in Houston's and get what your Mama said. I'm gonna pick up some feed and I'll just pull out front and pick you up." Daddy said as he handed me a five-dollar bill. "Bring me my change, but don't buy that cheap tape. You got to keep a bandage on that toe. Don't want it infected."

"No Sir," I said as I stepped out of the truck. The feeling was back now, and it hurt like crazy. I realized what Mama was saying. I certainly couldn't put a shoe on that foot.

I opened the door of Houston's Drug Store and continually looked down. I didn't want to bump anything with my toe and I really didn't want to explain what had happened.

I was maneuvering to the back of the store where Mr. Joyce Houston always greeted each customer. To this day, I remember Mr. Houston as one of the kindest, most gentle men I ever knew. He was a pillar in the Baldwyn community and was the epitome of customer service.

Long before I got to the counter for Mr. Houston to greet me, I heard a familiar voice. "Linda Joy, what in the world has happened to your foot?" There stood Mrs. Elizabeth Bishop starring at my white sock, a little blood stained and obviously covering a thick bandage around the big toe.

Elizabeth was the mother of Linda Bishop who was in my class.

"Oh Miss Elizabeth, I am so embarrassed. I can't wear a shoe on this foot and school starts Monday."

"What happened to your foot?"

How I hated to tell her, but I couldn't lie. So, I told her the whole story – probably more than she bargained for.

As if she read my mind she offered, "So, you think the city kids will laugh because a cow stepped on your toe?"

"Yes, ma'am 'sorta'."

"Well, let me tell you something, Linda Joy Gholston," and she leaned in for emphasis, "none of them own a cow!" It took a minute to soak in. She was spot on – none of them did own a cow. Wow! My outlook was totally different after that brief conversation!

I got what I needed. The tape was on sale, so I spent another nickel and got Keylon some Bit-o-Honey. He loved that candy!

Monday, I went to school with my sore, bandaged toe in a white sock ready for anyone who made light of my plight. No one did until lunch. A rather 'snotty' tenth grader said in a very condescending way, "Let your cow step on you, did you?"

I looked at her with Miss Elizabeth's facial expression as much as I could muster and simply asked: "How many cows do you own?"

Linda Gholston

Winter of '56

The winter of '56 was an exciting, yet often frightening time for our family. We were thrilled beyond description to have our newborn baby, Keylon Douglas. However, he was often sick, and I could tell Mama and Daddy worried about him. He had croup and asthma. Of course, our only source of heat was a wood burning fireplace and I'm sure that didn't help. Many nights Mama and Daddy would take turns staying awake to watch the baby. I would beg to take a turn, but they always reminded me of school and sent me to bed.

One Saturday morning when Keylon was less than three months old, he started getting congested. Mama gave him the medicine prescribed by Dr. Gene Caldwell and held him over steaming water by the stove. He seemed to improve slightly throughout the day.

Daddy came home about six o'clock from the CO-OP. Mama told him about Keylon, and Daddy asked, "Do you think we can go to Susie and LeRoy's tonight? I really hate to miss the boxing match."

Mama looked at Daddy like he had three eyes, "No. We are not getting this baby out in the night air. I'm trying to get him better. You milk and then take over. I'm give out."

Daddy just got the milk bucket and headed to the barn. I knew Mama was right, but I felt sorry for Daddy. He loved to watch wrestling and boxing on television. We went to Uncle LeRoy and Aunt Susie's house at least twice a week and sometimes three times. Tonight, we all would be staying home with a sick baby.

Monday, I got home from school to find the baby much better. Mama said, "We dodged a bullet."

Daddy came home about six and immediately picked up the baby. He was relieved to find Keylon breathing with ease.

"Went by Raymond Hill's today" he said to Mama.

"What for?" she asked.

"He had ordered some horse feed and I just took it down there to save him a trip."

Mr. Raymond Hill owned Hill's Appliances. Mama and Daddy had bought our stove and refrigerator from him.

"He had a good deal on a television, so I just bought us one. They'll deliver it tomorrow."

"You bought a television?" Mama said in disbelief.

"Yeah. I didn't go down there to buy one, but he just offered me such a good deal on this one, I couldn't turn it down." He had his milk bucket and was out the door.

I got home from school Tuesday afternoon and sitting catty cornered in our living room was a console TV. Oh my! We might not have an indoor toilet, but we would never miss wrestling or boxing again!!

Linda Gholston

Whiskey

Keylon continued to be very sick, very often, throughout his first few months. In fact, he was hospitalized when he was six weeks old. Dr. Gene Caldwell came into his room late one afternoon and said to Mama, "Trixie, I'm going to try something you won't like."

"What's that?" Mama asked.

"Whiskey."

"Whiskey?"

"Yes, ma'am. I'm going to send down to the liquor store and get some. Nothing else is helping this baby. He's a sick boy."

Mama started to cry, and I did, too. Daddy calmed us down and said, "Doc, you know best. Do whatever you think can help my boy." I heard Daddy's voice break a little. At this moment I was the most frightened I had ever been. We just huddled around the baby in total silence. I'm certain we were all praying.

Hambone, a kind black man who worked at Caldwell Clinic, opened the door in about ten minutes and handed Dr. Gene a brown paper bag and simply said, "Doc, here it is."

"Thank you, Hambone," Daddy offered.

Dr. Gene went outside the little hospital room. We were just across the hall from the utility area where nurses prepared medicines. I stood outside of Keylon's room and watched. Dr. Gene lit the Bunsen burner and turned the flame low. He saw me and began to explain. "We're going to put some of this whiskey in a spoon and hold it over this flame. We'll burn the alcohol off and then give your brother a drop after it's cooled." I watched. His steady hand held the spoon of whiskey over the burner and soon I saw a blue flame in the spoon. When the flame disappeared Dr. Gene put the content of the spoon into a  little dish. He stirred it gently. After a bit he said, "It's ready." Then he used a medicine dropper and syphoned the liquid into the glass tube. "Let's try this." He said.

Mama held Keylon and Dr. Gene put one drop into the baby's mouth. He stretched, made a face and finally swallowed. About fifteen minutes later, Dr. Gene repeated with another drop and instructed the nurse to give Keylon one drop every hour throughout the night.

Daddy took me to Ma and Pa Gholston's. Ma said a special prayer for Keylon that night and the early morning report was that he was some improved. After several days Keylon was home. There would be many bouts with bronchitis, asthma and tonsillitis during his early years, but none as severe as this one.

Linda Gholston

Mama's Prize

In January 1957, Keylon was four months old and no matter the weather, Mama, Daddy and I could watch TV. We got channel 9 (Tupelo) with no problem. To get channel 3 (Memphis), someone had to watch the TV, somebody had to stand at the door and somebody had to maneuver the antenna. Usually, Mama was the TV watcher; I stood at the door and transmitted her directions to Daddy who turned the antenna. "Rights" and "lefts" were often confused!

One night before Daddy got home, Mama and I were watching a local gospel group on channel 9. We had a big fire and Keylon was sound asleep. The announcer said, "We are about to play a beautiful instrumental. The first ten callers who can identify the song will win a very nice prize."

Seconds into the song, Mama said, "That's the 'Tennessee Waltz!' I know it is. You watch the baby. I'm going to Ozell's to call." (We didn't have a phone.) She was putting on a coat and wrapping her head in a scarf as she talked.

"Ok, Mama. Hope you're one of the ten!"

She grabbed the flashlight and walked hurriedly across the road to Mrs. Ozell's house. I was 'dreaming' of the prize. What could it be? A new TV? Free groceries? A trip? Seemed as if Mama was gone for an eternity.

Finally, the front door opened, and her breath vapor was like fog. She was shivering as she moved close to the fire and checked on the baby. He hadn't moved.

"Mama, did you win?"

"Yes, I won."

She didn't seem very happy. Actually, she seemed a little dejected.

"What was the prize, Mama?" I ventured.

"Fifty dollars off a vacuum cleaner. I was foolish to fall for that." I just hugged her and assured her we didn't need a vacuum cleaner.

Women of Substance

Looking at childhood now as one passed seventy-years-old is quite revealing. I would suggest the exercise for all, no matter the age. I realize now so much about the personalities, attitudes and reactions of those in my tiny world that I could not possibly have noticed as a child.

As children we haven't accumulated enough experiences to realize it is life's experiences and our reactions to them that mold us into the individuals, families, and communities that we become. I have come to realize that my family was totally human – 'warts' and all. Their strengths far outweighed their weaknesses, and their love for me is fundamental for my decisions, actions, and beliefs throughout my life.

When I was born in 1947, my family had experienced a couple of tragic years. They lost Uncle Marvin in 1945 and Elizabeth Ann in 1946. Mama, Daddy and both sets of grandparents were dealing with two tremendous losses, as well as Aunt Tannis' destructive coping mechanisms.

Ma Gholston would tell me, "You are a ray of sunshine." At the time I thought, as any self-centered child, the comment was all about me. Now, I realize that the comment was really about their healing and proof that life goes on.

I look back and see the influence of many, but two women in particular.

First, Ma Gholston. She was a woman of strong faith. When I was about twelve years old she began to open up and talk about Uncle Marvin. She missed him so. I remember one fall afternoon we were raking leaves in the front yard. Both of us loved piling them high, lighting the fire and watching them burn. The smell was warm and inviting, it just made me feel loved all over!

After we finished, we sat in two metal chairs in the front yard she and Pa usually kept reserved for company. She was tired and a little melancholy. She said, "Of all the kids, Marvin loved to rake and pile leaves. Why, I can hear him laughing now and jumping on the big piles. Did you know he had a dog?"

"No ma'am, I didn't."

"Well, every morning he would ask me to cook two extra biscuits for that dog." We didn't tell Papa. That dog had the shiniest coat from all the lard in the biscuits. He would wait on Marvin every afternoon to get home from school. My, my how he loved that dog."

There was a long silence. I didn't know what to say but I felt I was being introduced to Uncle Marvin and I liked him.

"Did I ever tell you about the vision God gave me after your Uncle Marvin died?"

"No ma'am."

"Well, I got a letter from Marvin telling me that he had accepted Jesus as his Savior and would be baptized as soon as possible."

[Ma and Pa attended Pratt Christian Church and believed that immersion was essential for salvation.]

"Soon after that letter we were informed of his death at twenty-three years old. Nothing hurts like losing a child."

I looked at Ma. She wasn't crying, just staring into a seemingly faraway place.

Then, she looked me in the eye and said, "God sent me a vision. Only one I ever had, only one I ever needed. A red bird was sitting outside the west window there in the front room; and it spoke to me."

"It did?"

"Yes, God sent the red bird to tell me that Marvin's soul is with Him. I miss Marvin terribly, but I don't grieve anymore. I know where he is. He can't come back to me, but I will, one day, go to him."

Ma took my hand and held it for the longest time. Total silence, yet deep communication. That afternoon I felt that I was Ma's friend. I loved being her granddaughter and I adored being her friend.

Another woman from my childhood that I greatly admired was my great aunt, Brevard Young Bailey. We called her Mama Brevard. She was Ma Butler's sister and lived with Mammie (their mother), Arnold Lee (her brother) and Belle (her daughter).

Mama Brevard's husband, Marlin died from malaria when their daughters, Lois and Belle were very young. Neither of them remembered their Daddy. She raised those girls never seeming to pity herself or think the world owed her anything.

When Mama Brevard was very sick with stomach cancer, I remember going to see her in the hospital as often as I could. One day I told her I was thinking about nursing school. Her thin, emaciated fingers were fiddling with the sheets. She stopped and looked at me with total clarity and simply said, "You've got what it takes." That declaration lodged in my heart of hearts and eventually, I would make it to nursing school. On the hardest days when I would think that I couldn't do it I would hear Mama Brevard say, "You've got what it takes." Although it was several years before I entered nursing school after Mama Brevard passed. My graduation would have been really special if she could have been there, but I felt her presence.

May all of us, like Ma Gholston and Mama Brevard, be encouragers. May we influence others to know their worth and assure them, "You've got what it takes."

Linda Gholston

Purse on the Bridge

Noel C. Butler was a prankster extraordinaire. In fact, he would tell us grandkids that his middle name was Cleveland on some days, on others he would say Chandler, and still on others he would say it was Candler. My cousin Joe is sure it was Chandler, cousin Becky thinks it was Cleveland. I'm not sure.

I am sure of this; he loved the outdoors, and he loved pulling pranks. He told me about several pranks he had pulled and taught me some to play on others.

One day I was at his house in the early spring and he was busy getting his fishing equipment all fixed up and ready to go. Every Friday afternoon he and his brother-in-law, Aude Woods, would try to catch a ride to Pickwick. Neither of them owned a vehicle, but somehow, they would get there, and they'd be home late Sunday in time for work on Monday morning. The first trip of the year was planned for the following week-end.

Big had a badly tangled line and was working patiently to get all the knots and tangles out.

"You wanta' help me?" He asked.

"Yes sir. I'll try. This stuff is invisible. How do you see it?"

"Don't. If you can see it, fish can see it. No good. You just have to feel it mostly," he said as he took a swig of hot coffee.

"They's lots of pranks you can pull with fishing line. I used to tie it between two trees and watch Aude fall when he was courtin' Clyter" (Big's sister was named Clyta but he called her 'Clyter' or 'Pete') "He's always been clumsy as all get out and he'd bust that ground open." Big laughed with a chuckle. "Took Aude fifteen minutes to get 'hisself' up and then Clyter would say, "Aude Woods, you're filthy. Why didn't you put on clean clothes?"

"I did Hon. Noel's up to his pranks," Aude would offer.

Big could do all the voices and sound just like the person he was imitating. (He called it mocking.) Aunt Susie inherited that skill. I loved to listen to her, especially when she imitated the song director and the preacher!

"I'll tell you a good trick you can do with fishing line," Big chuckled again at the thought. I always loved Big's ideas for tricks, so I was all ears.

He continued to untangle yards and yards of fishing line as he talked. "Ask your mama or Ma for one of their old purses. That part will be up to you, but I think Rosie bought a new one not long ago. Then, I'll give you fifty, maybe sixty yards of line. Tie one end around the handle of the purse and put it on the bridge. Run the line on the side, and you hide in the bushes by the bridge.

When someone stops and bends down to get the purse, you yank." We both got so tickled just thinking about reactions we might see.

Big gave me the line wrapped around a stick. Ma Butler gladly gave me her old purse. She said, "That thing is wore out. You can play with it." Little did she know what Big had taught me and the hours of fun my neighbor Larry and I would have.

The very next day I was ready. Larry and I fixed up the purse and walked through the pasture to the bridge. When no traffic was seen to the left or right, we eased the purse up and placed it on the edge of the bridge. We carefully unwound the fishing line, and holding it tightly we hid ourselves in some bushes near the bridge. Then, we heard it! A vehicle was coming! An old truck came chugging along. The man must have looked straight ahead because he never even slowed down. Larry climbed up to the bridge and moved the purse a little more toward the middle.

In about ten minutes we heard another vehicle, an old truck traveling east. It seemed that the driver spied the purse and instantly hit his brakes. We watched as he opened his door and stepped out of his truck. We were excited and yanked the purse before he got close to it.

That man just shook his head, seemed irritated and got back in his truck and chugged off.

It was getting late, a little dusky dark and we knew our mamas would be calling us in very soon. We hoped for one more vehicle.

We realized our mistake and would not prematurely pull the purse next time. Finally, a car came from the west. It was a woman driver. She saw the purse and stopped about twenty feet beyond it.

We watched and resisted pulling the purse while she was a distance away. When she was about two feet away and beginning to bend down, we yanked. The purse flew over the edge of the bridge. We stayed totally still and quiet.

She walked to the edge trying to see who did this. In an angry, high pitched voice she said, "Whoever y'all idiots are, you better be glad I got on hose and heels. If I didn't, I'd come down there and beat the *#*# out of y'all."

Larry and I looked at each other and she continued to rant and rave. No doubt we both learned some words that day.

This would be one of many spring and summer afternoons we would use this old straw purse and fishing line to pass the time.

Hog Killing Day

Hog killing day ranked right up there with Christmas and Fourth of July! It was a spectacle to behold. First, Pa Gholston would read the Farmers' Almanac while Daddy and Uncle Bulich listened to the weather on the radio. The decision would be tentatively decided about a week in advance and 'set in concrete' about forty-eight hours prior to the event. NASA had nothing on the Gholstons as they prepared for 'launch'. Ours didn't involve a rocket, just one rifle shot from a sharp shooter like Uncle Bulich.

Ma Gholston would spend much of the week prior to hog killing day making sausage sacks. She had saved the white cloth flour sacks and stitched them into tubes about three inches wide and sixteen inches long. She would use scraps of material to make ties for the tops. Also, she had to make sure she had plenty of salt, black pepper and red pepper. She and I would go to the well house to check on the big sack of dried sage. It smelled so good. Today when I smell sage I think of Ma's chicken and dressing, as well as hog killing day.

Pa spent the week getting the big black cast iron wash pot cleaned and ready. Then he and I would walk in the pasture and gather limbs to use for the fire. If he needed more, he would ask Daddy and Uncle Bulich to pull a few big limbs (logs) from the bottom. After this came Pa's most important job and the one I hated the most – he had to sharpen all the knives.

Every year he would tell me about his daddy falling dead while he sharpened a knife to kill hogs. I would watch Pa like a hawk, so afraid that he too would die while sharpening his knives. Thank goodness, he did not.

About four days before the actual event the decision makers would gather in the early morning. If weather was cooperating and all preparations were a 'go' they would take a bucket of corn and lure the hog into the barn. Once the chosen 'ham bearer' was in a stall, the door was latched tightly. Now, he would be fed nothing but corn, sweet feed, and water until his 'execution'. Pa and I would fill his trough twice a day and make sure he had plenty of water. That hog would 'chow down' on the corn, not realizing that in a few short days he would suffer a fatal shot between the eyes. How could something that smelled so bad taste so good?

At supper on the day before the hog killing, the air seemed electrified. Everyone was in a great mood and lots of questions were asked: "Do you have enough sacks for sausage?" "Is the smoke house cleaned out and ready?" "Do we have enough curing salt for the hams?" "Seasonings ready?" "Enough firewood?" A litany of questions and each one answered affirmatively. Someone would give the latest weather report: low tonight 28°, high tomorrow just 36° with a slight wind. No rain and low tomorrow night 27°. Pa would sit in silence as if he were placing each answer in the equation and then pronounce, "Boys, lets plan to start the fire at five in the morning, and Bulich, you have him shot by good daylight. That way we ought to be through 'fore dark'. Y'all know what happened to my daddy on hog killing day. If it happens to me, ya'll just go on with the killin'."

Uncle Bulich laughed, "Papa, you been telling us that since 'I's' a boy."

"Well, it's the truth", Pa would say. Seemed not to scare anybody except me.

I would sleep with Ma Gholston on this special night. I had the same trouble going to sleep that I had on Christmas Eve. It wasn't sugar plums dancing in my head; rather it was the thoughts of bacon, ham, and sausage that I would be enjoying.

Ma would quietly get out of bed at four-thirty. While she cooked breakfast, Pa would start a fire, so the front room would be warm. Then he would slip out into the dark morning and get the fire going for the wash pot. Cooking out the lard and making the cracklings was a major part of the day.

I would wake up early and run to the kitchen. "Have they shot it, Ma?"

"I hadn't heard the gun, so don't stick your head out. Get here by the fire. Breakfast will be ready 'd'rectly'."

I would see tractor and truck lights as neighbors began to gather. Pa, Daddy and Uncle Bulich helped them kill and dress their hogs, and our neighbors returned the favor.

Ma would send a plate of biscuits with meat and cups of hot coffee out for all the men folks gathered around Pa's big fire.

Most of them would say, "I et' fore I came, Ms. Phronnie", as they reached for a biscuit and cup of coffee. The women folk would come inside, eat a biscuit and prepare for a fun, productive day.

Mama would dress me in the warmest clothes I had, put on my coat, and cover my ears after she stuffed them with cotton. I had terrible earaches as a child, and she did what she could to prevent them. I was practically 'deaf' from the cotton stuffing, but out I went to face the cold wind and watch the 'happenings'. The hog was dead. Uncle Bulich and Daddy with the help of neighbors had chained the back legs of the hog and hoisted it in the air using the Ferguson tractor. Uncle Bulich moved the hog as close to the wash pot as possible.

By now, the water was boiling. Daddy would dip and pour a bucket of scalding water on the hog and all the men, with their pocket knives would begin to scrape. When they finished, all hair had been removed. Then Pa would say, "Let's portion this hog." An incision was made, and all internal organs were removed. They wasted nothing.

A man from west of Baldwyn was there for the intestines. He put them in a big bucket, so he and his family could have 'chitlins'. "Mr. Fate, I sure thank you and Ms. Phronnie. Will y'all come eat with us? We'll clean these good, season 'em up and fry 'em."

Pa laughed, "John, you know there's not much I don't like but y'all enjoy 'em. Tell Martha not to let you eat enough of them to make yourself sick." With Mr. John gone with the intestines, Daddy and Uncle Bulich removed the other internal organs. The liver went in a dish pan along with the heart. The stomach underside or pork belly was for bacon.

Ma Gholston washed the liver and heart and ground them, added onion, various peppers and seasoning and cooked the pork hash. Pa then took the bladder, washed it thoroughly and filled it with water. He carefully placed it on a stick and said to me, "Here's you a balloon. Don't take it in the house but play all you want to outside." A pig bladder balloon!

On a long table, the men cut the hog into parts. There were hams, shoulders, tenderloin, and other tasty cuts of meat. The fat was put in Pa's big black pot and the lard was rendered. (Cooked until it totally liquified) The rind was crispy. We loved salted pork rind (cracklings) as a snack with parched peanuts. Very good!!

Sausage was made by grinding the lean and the fat together with salt, red pepper, and sage. After the dish pan was full Ma would stop and fry a few pieces. We would take them out for the men to sample. Everybody was free to eat, but only Pa made the decision. Whatever he suggested got added and mixed. Another round of frying sausage. Usually, he pronounced it "perfect" after the second round. Thank goodness!

The hot grease was poured into a large lard can, allowed to cool and then sealed and placed on the back porch. The pork rinds were ladled out into a cardboard box and liberally salted. Everybody dug in!

The day after the hog killing after the brain had been removed, Ma would put the hog's head in a big pot of water and cook it for several hours. All of the meat would be tender and succulent. Ma would season it with sage and peppers and press into a deep oblong pan. She would press it firmly, wrap it securely and put a brick on the top. It stayed in the frig untouched for one week. She would open it like a great gift and there would be delicious souse meat for sandwiches.

There were so many highlights associated with hog killing time! I have to close with this: Breakfast the morning after was a traditional feast for the entire family. Ma's homemade, "light as a feather" biscuits, fresh sausage, and homespun butter with Ma's fig preserves were on the table. The center piece was a big, gigantic bowl of hog brain and eggs. They were not appetizing. I didn't want to eat them.

Pa would put a large serving on his plate and pass the bowl to me with this assertion: "If you eat these brains and eggs, you'll be mighty smart."

My portion might not equal his, but it wasn't small. I sure wanted to be smart. Uncle Bulich and Aunt B would laugh quietly, shake their heads but pass on the brains and eggs. Eating them didn't make me smart, but it made my Pa Gholston happy! Good enough for me.

The smokehouse sat back of the kitchen. We stepped out of the kitchen backdoor onto a walkway that seemed to me to have been about three feet wide and five or six feet long and about five feet off the ground. There were not steps to the ground, only to the door of the smokehouse. Once inside it was dark, cold and smelled of meat at different stages of maturing.

On each inside of the smokehouse, Pa and Uncle Bulich had built sturdy, wall attached trays to hold hams. These were covered in curing salt. Cracks were purposefully left in the tray bottoms, so blood and juices could freely drip from the curing meat. As the salt became blood stained it would be removed and replaced by fresh salt. The hams were fragrant and salty once they were ready to eat. A lot of time and effort went into making it so delectable. After Ma fried a big skillet of country ham she would add strong coffee and black pepper to the drippings. Nothing better than red-eye gravy and a biscuit! Mama and Daddy continued to enjoy red-eye gravy all their lives, though less frequently as they aged.

My family continues to gather on Christmas Eve morning for breakfast. The menu varies but biscuits and ham with red-eye gravy is a constant. Hope it will always be…a Gholston tradition.

The shoulders were hung from the ceiling with thick ropes as they needed to drip their juices, but they were not salt cured. Same for the sacks of sausage. The pork belly was cut in slabs and laid back of the hams; they were lightly salted. Curing followed the same process as the hams. Best bacon ever!

Pa and Ma Gholston's smoke house served its purpose, but I have to admit I enjoyed eating the meat more than 'tending it' as it cured.

Now, Big Daddy's smokehouse was a different venture from Pa Gholston's. He smoked his meat, and I loved that process! I don't remember ever getting to be with them on an actual hog killing day, but I vividly recall him smoking the meat.

His smokehouse sat several yards from his back porch. Same design as Pa Gholston's. I guess they all were.

Big would gather hickory wood and once he got his pork shoulders roped and Ma Butler got the sausage sacks stuffed, they would hang them in the smokehouse. He always wanted one ham to eat "green." Ma Butler would boil it for a while and then bake it. It was so very good with potatoes, green beans and corn bread. The other hams and the pork belly he would salt cure.

The fun was seeing Big Daddy pull his big black pot into the center of his smokehouse which had a dirt floor. He would put kindling in the bottom of the pot and then his hickory. He would light the fire and get it blazing. To create a lot of smoke, he would gently lower a wet blanket onto the pot. Smoke would billow!

Big would close the door tightly and soon smoke would begin to curl out of the cracks of the smokehouse. He would check it frequently and add more hickory wood and dampen his blanket again. The aroma was fine, and the smoked sausage was 'divine'!

Linda Gholston

Goats

The piercing pain started about four o'clock one afternoon in late October. It wasn't the first bout and certainly wouldn't be the last. Mama immediately warmed the sweet oil and put a dropper full in my right ear. She had one of Daddy's socks filled with salt, and she put it near the fire to heat.

I was about five years old. I screamed and cried until the oil numbed the pain or I just became too tired to cry. Daddy rocked me and kept a good fire going. About midnight he put me in the bed. I slept until three-thirty in the morning. Mama told Daddy to stay in bed, she would rock me.

She added wood to the fire, bundled us up in a thick quilt after she dropped more oil into my ear canal. At her encouragement I was as quiet as possible, so Daddy could sleep. Mama sang all the old hymns, such as: *Amazing Grace, Near the Cross, Nothing but the Blood and Just as I Am.*

Daddy got up at five-thirty and stoked the fire. Mama and I were dozing. He warmed the salt sock and took me in his arms, so Mama could cook breakfast. About six-thirty we ate, and I heard a horn blowing out front. Daddy told me that he was going to the sale barn with Mr. Clovis Mink. Daddy had two good heifers and one bull to sell.

Even after paying Mr. Clovis the "hauling fee" and the "auctioneer fee" at the sale barn, Daddy felt he would make good money.

He hated to leave Mama and me in that old drafty house, but he wanted to get those animals to the sale barn. These three he had raised, so his profit margin stood to be significant. As he was leaving he said, "I hope your ear gets better. I'll try to bring you something." With that he was out the door.

Periodically throughout the day, the piercing pain would occur. Mama kept the drops warm by the fire, as well as the salt sock. We rocked, and she sang a lot that day.

I was in Mama's lap when we heard Mr. Clovis' pick-up and saw the lights as they turned in about six o'clock. Almost as soon as we saw them we realized Mr. Clovis was turning to head out. Mama said, "I bet your Daddy got you a candy bar."

"I hope so."

About then we heard the front door open and immediately the door into our room. I was snuggled up on Mama enjoying being pain free for a few minutes. My right ear was on the salt sock against Mama, and I didn't want to move.

Suddenly, Mama said, "Douglas, what have you done?"

Daddy quickly replied, "I got her a goat!"

With cat like reflexes I jumped up from my soft warm spot and looked at Daddy. He sat a tiny white goat in the floor. The goat just stood there; I just sat on Mama's lap. I was expecting a candy bar and got a goat!

"What do you think?" Daddy asked.

"I like him. What's his name?" I asked.

Daddy said, "Well, it's a boy so I guess we'll call him Billy." (Not much originality when it came to naming our animals.)

In a few seconds, Billy began to run all over the house. I chased him until my ear hurt again. I climbed back into Mama's lap and our "ear ache" routine began again. Daddy put Billy in a little enclosure on the back porch of the Whitlock house.

We all enjoyed more sleep that night, and the next day Billy and I began a friendship that would last for over a year. He really was a family pet who loved to play chase. I didn't have other children for playmates at that time, but Billy and I were inseparable!

When Billy was about one and a half years old he slipped out of the barn one day into the pasture. There were cows and calves, so he didn't want for companionship.

Something no one anticipated happened the next week. Mr. Luther Whitlock was fertilizing his field that ran to the edge of the pasture. The fences were good, and Billy couldn't get out, but a couple of fertilizer sacks blew against the fence. His goat nature was to eat any paper he could find. So, Billy pulled the sacks through the fence and began to nibble. Of course, the fertilizer was poisonous to a goat.

Daddy found Billy late that afternoon. He was very bloated and dead. We buried Billy and I cried. I remember being so angry at Mr. Whitlock, who would never intentionally hurt an animal.

Daddy asked me a few days later if I wanted another goat. My Uncle Lawrence Roper had a new litter of boxer bulldogs, and he promised me one of those. So, I told Daddy I would soon have my puppy and we just wouldn't risk another goat getting into the fertilizer.

Years later, about six weeks before my niece Lakin's eighth birthday I asked her what she wanted Aunt Linda to give her. She answered as quickly as I asked, "A goat!"

"Lakes, you want a goat for your birthday?"

"Yes, I do, and Mama and Daddy said it's ok. So, will you get me a goat?"

"Well, I'll try to find some goats. We'll see," I told her.

"Aunt Linda, you had a goat, and I really want one, too. Please."

My heart melted as I thought back to Billy and the fun we had. Soon I learned that Doris Harkey had goats. Doris and I had been in high school together, so I knew it would be fun to visit with her and her husband, Paul.

I called, and Doris said, "sure, I have goats for sale." Lakin and I planned to go to Doris' on Saturday afternoon. It was late August and hot as blue blazes. I'm thinking fifteen minutes at the most and we will be headed home. Wrong!

We got in Doris' barn with about twenty goats. Green flies were everywhere. For all the interest I didn't have in this herd of goats, Lakin was overflowing with interest. Doris pointed out the three that were for sale.

After two and a half hours, Lakin just couldn't decide. "Aunt Linda, when can we come back?"

"I'll be home in two weeks. (I was living in Jackson, Mississippi at this time.) We can come then if it's ok with Doris. It was.

Two weeks later we were back in the same barn. It was just as hot as two weeks before, and the flies had multiplied. The three "for sale" goats hadn't changed a lot.

Lakin had read a great deal about goats and began to point out the characteristics of each one. She sounded then a lot like the veterinarian she is today. Doris said she really didn't like for people to purchase one of her goats and change the name. So, she proceeded to tell Lakin each name and its origin.

I thought, "Who is crazier here? Lakin for spending such an inordinate amount of time selecting a goat? Doris for having so many goats with well-chosen names? Or, could it be me? The aunt for tolerating this long, elaborate discussion on goat sizes, temperaments, genetics, etc."

Then, I recalled Daddy's smile when I saw Billy. At that moment Lakes said, "Aunt Linda, I choose Kristen. We'll have fun like you and Billy."

Today, Lakin's son, Trevor, who is two already has three goats. His favorite by far is Tina. So, in our animal linage there will always be Billy, Kristin and Tina.

Wisdom

When Keylon was in the third grade it was obvious he was exceptionally bright. He read well and excelled in math. His teachers praised his ability and called him "an excellent student."

One night Daddy told Keylon to get his lessons. I don't know if Keylon didn't feel well, was tired or had just had a bad day. Out of the blue he calmly announced, "I hate school. I hate studying. When I get grown I'm going to buy a motorcycle, wear a leather jacket, and milk cows for Mr. Odene."

Mr. Odene Grissom was a great guy, a wonderful friend to my Daddy, a farmer who milked a large herd of cattle. He spent a lot of time with Keylon showing him his milking operation. As an eight-year-old, Keylon wanted to grow up and work with Mr. Odene.

I couldn't believe what I'd just heard Keylon say. So, I jumped in 'with both feet'. "You are not going to milk cows for a living!"

"Yes, I am and ride a motorcycle," He retorted.

"No, you are not! You are very smart. God has given you a good mind and you cannot 'waste' yourself milking cows."

"I told you I'm working for Mr. Odene. You don't run my life," Keylon said in a huff.

"You will get killed riding that motorcycle."

"No, I won't. I love motorcycles."

This banter between Keylon and me went on for a while. Finally, I said, "Daddy, tell him he can't do that. He can't wear a black leather jacket, ride a motorcycle and milk cows. He's too smart, Daddy, you tell him."

Daddy, very matter of factly said, "Son, Odene expects his hands to be there ready to milk by four o'clock every morning. If you are going to ride a motorcycle it'll be mighty cold in the winter. A 'fer piece' over there. And, you'll have to be back there at four every evening to milk again."

"Yes, Sir. I know that, Daddy," Keylon said as he stared at me.

"Well, son if you're going to work for Odene give him an honest day's work for an honest day's pay."

"I will Daddy and that's what I'm 'gonna' do."

"Ok son. Now get your lessons," Daddy said.

That was the end of the conversation. Keylon got his books and stretched out on the floor by the fire and began to read. How could Daddy be so wrong and me be so right? I really felt smugly proud of myself for the lecture I'd given to Keylon.

After about an hour had passed Keylon went to get a shower. Finally, I could, hopefully, help Daddy see the error of his way and get him to straighten Keylon out before bedtime.

"Daddy, why didn't you agree with me? You know Keylon is too smart to waste his life milking cows?"

Daddy was sitting by the fire slowly peeling an apple for his bedtime snack. He always was meticulous with an apple, peeling carefully to have only one long, curled peel when he finished.

"Oh, I suspect he'll change his mind, but if he don't it's important that he's on time and does a good job. Now, don't talk anymore about this to him. Let's see what he thinks in a few years."

How could Daddy be so wrong about something I wondered, but I didn't say another word. Over the years as I watched Keylon mature and grow, I realized Daddy's wisdom. After third grade I never heard him mention milking cows again. He was going to be a wrestler, a cowboy, a professional football player; all by the ninth grade.

Years after that conversation, my nephew Douglas Clay, Keylon and Teresa's youngest son, was talking with me one afternoon on the deck at Mama's and Daddy's. It was just the two of us and Clay, at about six and a half years old said, "Aunt Linda, I know what I want to do when I'm grown."

"You do, what's that?"

"Well, something about bull 'ridin,'" Clay said.

My Daddy's wisdom clicked in. "Really? What are you going to do?"

"I don't exactly know," Clay said. "I'm not 'gonna' ride the bull. That's for sure way too dangerous. I don't want to be that clown in a barrel either. That bull butts that barrel a long ways. I think I'll be the one that opens the gate. What do you think about that?"

Trying to sound and think like Daddy I said, "Clay that's a very important job. You can't be one second too fast or one second too slow. It's really an important job."

With a smile as wide as Texas, Clay said, "Yep, that's what I'm 'gonna' do."

Keylon and Clay both went on to receive Master's Degrees at Mississippi State University. Today, Keylon is the Cotton Product Manager for Monsanto and Clay is a Crop Consultant with Crop Production Services. Their aspirations and dreams have changed with time. So, has my wisdom! It will never equaled my parents, but was a lot more sound with Clay than with Keylon.

Linda Gholston

Values

Writing this book has not been the chore I dreaded it to be. It has been a joy! I began this journey of recording early childhood remembrances thinking primarily of those who would read it. I was wondering if my nieces and nephews and especially my great nieces and nephews could identify with peddling trucks, hog killings, pranks that involved magic eggs, purses on a bridge and the old rotary dial phones that came with party lines?

A short distance into the writing, my focus changed. I went back in time and enjoyed visits with those from my past as I recalled events. Ma Gholston's generosity and goodness flooded my soul. When Ma died I was a teenager and I thought her influence ended there. Of late, I have come to realize that she and countless others continue to offer me aspirations to improve and be a better human being.

From Pa Gholston I learned the value of routine and now understand why he talked often of death. In one month's time he lost his two loving sisters, Aunt Hattie and Aunt Carrie, and his son, Marvin. Can you imagine the heartache and grief in a time span of thirty days? I look now with such admiration. In spite of his heartache, he found plenty of time and energy to love on and mold his grandchildren.

Ma Butler and Big Daddy dealt with their share of adversity also. Through it all, Ma continued to have great pride in her dress and her house. She may have seen the glass half empty, but that woman could bake a tea cake like no one else.

Today when I eat Joe Butler's tomato soup it certainly takes me back to Ma Butler's little kitchen table with an oil cloth covering and her pouring up a steaming bowl of tomato soup with hot cornbread. She would always say, "Your Uncle Marvin loved this soup."

As serious as Ma Butler was, Big Daddy was jovial and fun loving. If he wasn't spinning a yarn, he was thinking up a prank. What I would give to be on their back porch one more time and see Big coming home with his lunchbox after a hard day's work on the Lee County roads. Becky and I would open that rounded top lunchbox immediately, with Ma Butler saying, "Don't eat that. It's been in the sun all day. Y'all will be a might sick." I don't think we ever intended to eat, although I'm not sure. I think we just wanted to smell the scent of his ham and biscuit mingled with coffee. Also, there lingered the faintest hint of one of Ma's famous fried pies.

Of course, the two people who influenced Keylon and me the most were Mama and Daddy. They were an ordinary couple with little education but tremendous wisdom. They stayed the course. During abundant crops and failed crops their commitment to hard work and caring for us never wavered. With the price of milk up and down, they continued to milk their cows. By their example, Keylon and I learned lessons galore and never realized, at the time, we were being schooled. These are the best lessons of life.

When I was seven, Mama used a switch and a circling of the barn to drive home a lesson I needed. I pray I've always lived that lesson. She and Daddy had spent a Saturday in the bottom land hoeing corn. It had been a very wet early summer and Johnson grass was getting taller than the corn. Daddy came in late on Friday and said, "I believe we can hoe that corn, at least around the edges tomorrow. If we don't get a break in this weather soon, we gonna' lose this corn crop. I'll step down to Papa's and see if Bulich can hoe after his milk route tomorrow."

Mama was fixing supper and said, "I'll cook extra biscuits in the morning and fix a big jug of water. That way, we won't have to come out of the field to eat."

About twenty minutes later Daddy reappeared. "Yep. Bulich will come straight to the field. Said he'd start his milk route about two-thirty and should join us by eleven-thirty. You better cook him about six biscuits. We got anything to put in them?"

"We got plenty of jelly and I'll fry what sausage I've got. It'll be a plenty."

With that, we ate supper quickly and Daddy went to the shop to sharpen the hoes. Tomorrow was going to be a tiring day. Chopping and pulling Johnson grass out of corn with the ground muddy and soured. Had to be done.

As I got ready for bed Mama said, "We'll leave at sun up for the bottom. I'll let Buster in." Buster Brown was my two-year-old boxer, and nobody would bother me with Buster around.

"I will pour your glass of milk and leave it in the 'frig'. Breakfast will be in the oven. Eat and then go to Ma's. Your clothes 'is' on the dresser. Don't dally."

"No ma'am."

About five o'clock Saturday afternoon Mama came walking into Ma Gholston's yard. She was leaning on her hoe handle.

"Trixie, you're exhausted," Ma said, "must be mighty hard working that corn out in this mud."

"Yes'um it is. We've got a lot done. Douglas and Bulich 'is' gonna hoe til dark. I come in to start milking. Come on, Linda Joy, let's drive the cows up and get started."

I told Ma good-bye. Mama and I found the two milk cows over behind the old Taylor house place. We walked behind the cows and drove them to the barn. Mama got her milk bucket and filled it about half full of hot water to wash the teats. It was hot in the barn, so I went outside to play.

Our barn was on a hillside (about where my house sits now). I could see across our pasture and also into Mr. Gordon Mabry's pasture where his share cropper house sat. Mr. Godfrey Watson and his family lived there. His daughter, Judy, who had flaming red hair and a bright smile, would come to the house to play sometimes. She was probably a couple of years older than I was, but we loved playing together.

Now, at seven I knew enough about wealth and status to be dangerous – real dangerous in Mama's and Daddy's eyes. I knew Daddy built our house and I knew Mr. Watson was a share cropper. From that I drew an extremely unhealthy, inaccurate conclusion.

As I stood there, a seven year old alone, I looked for several minutes at the Watson scene. There must have been twenty kids playing chase, Bobby Watson and a friend of his were playing guitars and someone was on the front porch churning homemade ice-cream.

When it became more than I could bare, I marched into the barn and stood in the doorway of the stall where Mama was milking. Just as I walked up to make my proclamation, the cow's tail swished Mama in the face. At that moment I said, "I sure do wish we 'was' poor folks like them Watsons."

My Mama sprang from that milking stool like she was shot from a cannon. I could tell I had said the wrong thing. She came out of the barn, got a switch from a tree (in my back yard now) and we began to circle the barn. Mama was hot, tired and mad. In this condition she gave a whipping like, well, like you never want! Once my legs were striped and she had my attention she screamed, "What do you mean? We are poor folks. Me and your daddy slave on this farm and this is the thanks we get?"

"Mama", I cried, "I didn't mean nothing bad. I just wish we had ice-cream, guitars, and a bunch of kids to play with."

"Well let me tell you, young lady, you don't ever say anything like that again. Do you hear me?"

"Yes, ma'am."

"We'll discuss this after your daddy gets in."

"Ok. I'm sorry. I love Judy and the Watsons."

"You better love them and everybody else." She went back to her milking and left me with a better understanding of what not to say.

We ate milk and bread for supper. We all washed up from the daily labor. Mama and Daddy sat out front under a big shade tree hoping to relax and feel a little breeze.

"Linda Joy, tell your daddy what you said while 'I's' milking."

"Well, Daddy, I told Mama I wished we 'was' poor like the Watsons. I didn't mean nothing bad. Just wishing I was having fun like they 'was'. I know we own our house and they don't." I started to cry.

Daddy pulled me on his lap and held me close for a while. "Linda, you are right about the houses. But, Honey, we are poor folks. Nobody is better than you or worse than you because of what they've got. Always work hard to improve your lot in life but don't ever look down on those that have less."

Reflecting on life, this may have been one of the most valuable talks Daddy and I ever had. I hope it can be said of me that my respect for others is not contingent on wealth, station in life or appearances. If God in His infinite wisdom created a being, who am I to pretend to lessen or increase their value?

Linda Gholston

House on Fire

Mama wore a sleeveless, thin, old shirt to drive the cows up for milking. She was very pregnant, and it was extremely hot. "This has been one of the worse days I've had" she said to no one in particular, but I was the only one around. She just didn't know how much worse the day would end.

We tended to things, ate supper, and Daddy got a bath. He had just come to the living room wearing clean Khakis and an undershirt. He didn't bother to put on shoes and socks as we would soon be going to bed. We thought.

A car turned into the driveway with the horn constantly sounding. Daddy jumped up and went outside barefoot. Mama and I were right behind him. With the windows rolled completely down a voice I didn't recognize said, "Doug, I'm headed to Friendship. There's a house on fire. Fraid it's Noel's." With that, he put his vehicle in reverse and threw rocks as he quickly backed out of the drive.

Mama started crying uncontrollably. Daddy dashed into the house and grabbed his shoes. He jumped in the pick-up as he talked to Mama. "You can't go, Trixie. It wouldn't be good for you or the baby. I'll be back as soon as I can." He looked at me and added, "Take care of your Mama." With that he left driving faster than I had ever seen.

Mama and I walked to the west end of the house. We could see a billowing black smoke and occasionally a blaze. "That's Mama's and Daddy's house. I've looked across that bottom too many times." No phone or any other way to know for certain but Mama knew.

Finally, we sat on the front porch and waited for Daddy. About eleven o'clock he got out of the truck and was covered with ash and soot. He just dropped down beside us and began, "Mr. Noel and Mrs. Rosie are ok. They were at Mammie's. Best we can tell, lost everything."

Mama cried hard. "What will they do? How's Mama? Are you sure they're ok - not hurt? I want to go."

"Your Daddy said for us to come in the morning. He's worried about you and the baby. Let's lay down and you try to rest. I'll milk early, and we'll go," Daddy said with a heavy voice from all the smoke and the heartache.

Mama just stared in space and nodded her head. Daddy took his clothes off and bathed again. He laid those filthy pants across a chair and said, "I'll put these back on in the morning. Lot to do to help your Big Daddy and Ma."

When I woke up early the next morning Daddy was already out of the house and Mama was making biscuits. I could tell she hadn't slept. Without really looking at me she said, "Put your clothes on and get ready to eat. Do you want to go over to Friendship with me and your daddy or stay with Ma Gholston?"

"I want to go see Ma and Big Daddy."

"Ok. There will be crying all day and lots to do. Such a loss. I don't know what Mama and Daddy will do."

"They could stay with us."

"Yes. I hope they will, but I doubt it."

About that time Daddy came in the house wearing those same filthy pants he had on last night. Smelling that smoke seemed to remind Mama again that her childhood home was gone.

We pulled into Ma's and Big's drive before seven o'clock that morning. Burned lumber was smoldering and ash was everywhere. Big walked to the truck and held Mama a long time. They both cried. He and Daddy shook hands and embraced. Daddy's voice was shaky as he said, "Mr. Noel, we'll get thru this together. Y'all are welcome at our house for as long as you need."

Big hugged me and just said, "Your ma is getting a little sleep at Brevard's."

All of the family and several neighbors gathered by nine o'clock. Everybody was just walking and looking while shaking their heads. I was witnessing shock. It was sinking in but had not totally sunk in. Ma Butler, Mama, Aunt Susie, and Aunt Tannis would seem fine one minute and burst out crying the next minute.

I just tried to stay close to Big Daddy. Ma seemed to have her daughters, sisters, and neighbors but Big seemed to have an unbearable weight on him. He squatted down in the front yard with a stick and began to draw. When he finished he said to Daddy and Uncle LeRoy, "This is what we'll build." He had drawn a much smaller house consisting of a small living room and bedroom with a fairly large kitchen. Off the kitchen was a back porch. The house was basically a rectangle sectioned in rooms for the various functions.

All afternoon and for days to follow, people came from all over the county to see Ma and Big. I noticed man after man shake hands with Big and leave a folded bill in his hand. They would all say basically the same thing, "Noel, I'll never forget what you did for me and my family" and, each would recount Big Daddy's kindness. It might have been something as simple as them remembering the way he graded their driveway and road that caused them to be so generous. My Big Daddy, because of his skill and love for others, dug more graves than any man in Lee County and would never accept payment. During his loss, he found that his goodness and grace were not forgotten.

Within a few months, Big Daddy, with the help of so many, had the little house he had drawn on the ground built in the same spot where the old house stood. Because so many blessed him, he and Ma paid cash, and neighbors gave them furniture for their new, little house.

Big's sister, Clyta or 'Clyter' as he called her gave them Big Daddy's Mama's twin spool beds. I have them now and treasure the rich family history they represent.

At eight I witnessed several valuable lessons when Ma's and Big's house burned:

1). Material things can be gone in an instant.

2). Be good to others from a heart of love and when you least expect, gifts will flood to you.

3). Even in tragedy, retain your jovial spirit. Big Daddy did.

Linda Gholston

Buster

"Uncle Lawrence, Maggie's belly sure is fat," I said during an October visit with Aunt Tannis and Uncle Lawrence.

"She's gonna' find puppies," he answered.

"Find puppies? Where?"

"In the barn, I imagine."

"Can we find'em?"

"No, that'll take Maggie girl, but it won't be long."

He would never use the word 'pregnant' and I would not have known its meaning. I was barely five and very naïve.

"I meant to keep it a surprise, but you're getting one of Maggie's pups," he said with a broad smile.

"I am?"

"Yes ma'am. Done asked your Mama and Daddy and they said it'd be ok. The daddy dog belongs to Teddy Scott. He'll get pick of the litter and then you can choose yours. Will be mighty good for you to grow up with a boxer bulldog. They're mighty protective of young'uns."

Wow!! In a few seconds I had gone from commenting on Maggie's big stomach to learning I was getting a puppy of my very own. Life can surely change quickly. I rode home later that day with Mama and Daddy, still in a fog of excitement that I was going to have a boxer.

The puppies were born that very night, but I didn't see Uncle Lawrence and Aunt Tannis for about three weeks. It was a Sunday at Ma and Big's for dinner that I saw them.

"Guess what, Peep-a-Boo?" Uncle Lawrence said.

"What? Did Maggie find'em puppies?"

"She did," he grinned ear to ear. "'They's' two girls and four boys. All healthy and eatin' good. Teddy will be out in a few days to get his pick and then you can pick yours from the remaining five.

Goodness! I was so excited. I told Ma and Big Daddy all about my puppy although I'd never seen it.

The following Saturday Mama and I rode Mr. Guy Mink's bus to Tupelo. My right foot turned inward, and Dr. Caldwell told Mama I needed some high top, lace up shoes from the Corner Shoe Store.

No matter what it was, if Keylon or I needed it, Mama and Daddy saw to it we had it. At an early age we both learned the difference in "need" and "want".

I remember us walking from the bus to the Corner Shoe Store. Going into the store, I saw an advertisement for Buster Brown shoes. (I couldn't read, therefore I didn't know what it said.) It was a picture of a little girl and her dog. I didn't say anything.

A nice man listened to Mama about my foot problem and then measured my feet. "Mighty narrow", he said. Then he went over and pulled a box from the shelf. He sat in front of me and laced the white shoes.

"These are perfect for her," he said as he patted my feet. "Buster Brown is the best brand on the market for long, narrow feet like hers."

Mama bought the shoes. The same picture was on the shoe box. We looked around a bit and then returned to Mr. Mink's bus.

On the ride home I ventured, "Mama, could I name my puppy Buster Brown?"

"If you get a boy puppy, you can," she answered and hugged me close to her.

Two weeks later on Wednesday afternoon Daddy told Mama, "I saw Lawrence in Baldwyn this morning. He said 'em puppies are eating good and Linda Joy can get hers anytime. He bobbed the tails last week. It's raining so we might as well go before supper if Bulich ain't using his truck."

"Suits me," Mama said. "I'd love to run up and see Mama and Daddy if we have time. We'll be so close."

Daddy was back for Mama and me in a few minutes. Thank goodness Uncle Bulich didn't need his pick-up truck. It was raining so hard and the roads were terribly muddy. About the time we pulled into Uncle Lawrence and Aunt Tannis' drive the rain reduced to a sprinkle. Aunt Tannis saw us and met us on the front porch. We all headed to the barn. Maggie and her beautiful pups were wagging 'nubby' tails and greeting their visitors. Maggie and Buster had no idea they were about to be a mama and son separated.

All the adults sat on bales of hay while I played with the five puppies. Buster was my favorite immediately. He gave me kisses and didn't run into the cow stall when I squealed. Finally, Daddy said, "Pick the one you want. We got to go see Ma and Big Daddy and then I've got to milk."

I held Buster up to Daddy and asked, "Is this a boy?"

He turned him over and said, "Yep, that's' a boy ok. He's pretty, too. Bet he'll make a fine pet."

I hugged Aunt Tannis and Uncle Lawrence and we loaded into the truck with Buster! Ma and Big Daddy really liked Buster Brown. Ma had tea cakes and I'd take a bite and give Buster a bite until Mama said, "Don't feed that puppy sweets. You'll give him the squirts."

We got home and Mama fixed Buster a bed in a big box on the covered back porch. I played with him as late as I could, but Daddy made it very clear that the dog would sleep outside.

I awoke on Thursday morning and ran immediately to the big back porch. Buster was fine. Mama had given him a saucer of milk and he was ready to play. Even the down pour of rain couldn't dampen my spirits. Buster and I were becoming fast friends.

Before dinner time I asked Mama if I could take Buster for Ma and Pa Gholston to see. "Oh no! Not in this weather," she said. "He's liable to take cold and die. We got to keep him warm and dry." The rain continued to pelt from the sky. I begged and begged, to no avail.

About three o'clock I decided to try again. Mama said no. She explained the puppy was too young. About thirty minutes later, Buster was in his box asleep and Mama said, "If you want to put on your boots and slicker (that's what we called a rain coat) you can go see Ma and Pa. Just come back before dark." It was just across the cotton patch.

As I walked, I had to think of some way to get them to see my puppy. I looked and saw Aunt B's car going down the drive. How could I get her to the house? Then an idea hit my mind!

Two nights before, Lois and Curtis Glenn had come to tell Mama and Daddy that Mr. Franklin, our distant neighbor, had gotten drunk and 'beat' Ms. Franklin. They talked about it for the longest time. How horrible it was!

So, not to be out done, I took off running as fast as I could. I ran in the house yelling, "Help! Help!

"What's wrong?" Aunt B asked looking stunned.

"Daddy is beating Mama"!

"What?"

"Come quick!"

She flew in the front door of our house. Hearing the commotion, Mama walked into the hallway.

"Trixie are you ok?"

"Yeah. Why?"

"Where's Douglas?"

"At the sale barn with Clovis Mink. Why?"

I stepped between them and said, "Aunt B, look at my puppy." She, of course, told Mama why she was so upset.

Oh my! Not a smart decision on my part.

Mama was scared, embarrassed and mad. Aunt B went home. Buster went to his box, and I got a spanking. This was sixty-five years ago, and I still remember it well. I never saw my Daddy strike my Mama and after this, I never said again that I did.

Buster eventually met Ma and Pa Gholston. Actually, he and I spent a lot of time with them. Pa said, "That dog is better protection than a Colt 45. How well I remembered the day he was 'no protection' at all!"

Linda Gholston

Lois and Billy Graham

When Robert and I were about twelve we loved playing pranks. Often times these involved the telephone. We would dial a number at random and just carry on a conversation by asking, "Do you know who this is?" As soon as they would guess, we would agree and just talk away. Should have been spanked and would have been, had any adults known about these telephone pranks.

One weekend Robert, Patricia, and their parents came from Starkville with plans for Robert and Patricia to spend the following week on the farm with us.

On Monday with most all adults working, Pa under the shade tree and Ma cooking, Robert and I got the two little ones (Keylon & Patricia) interested in something outside, and we quietly slipped into the front room where the telephone was ready for us to pull another trick.

I told Robert that Curtis and Lois Glenn had come to our house three nights the week before to watch the Billy Graham Crusade. It really was like church in our living room. Mama and

Lois loved to hear George Beverly Shea singing and one-night Ethel Waters sang, "His Eye is on the Sparrow". Lois cried.

So, we rehearsed our prank with Robert pretending to be the man from the radio station and me being Lois.

Then we dialed Lois' number. It was about ten o'clock am and I knew she was cooking dinner. Curtis would be home about fifteen minutes before noon from the field. Lois was a wonderful cook and like Ma, had homemade dessert at every meal.

After just two rings, she said, "Hello."

Robert paused, lowered his voice as much as possible and told her some fictitious name and that he was with WELO in Tupelo.

"Do 'ya listen' to our station?" he asked.

"Sometimes I do, but mostly I listen to the Booneville station. They 'got' more gospel programs than y'all do."

We wanted to roll with laughter but kept our composure. Robert then asked, "Mrs. Glenn, did you happen to see the Billy Graham Crusade last week?"

"I'll tell you the truth, we 'seen' three nights. Curt was just too late in the field and milking the other nights."

"Did you enjoy it?"

"Oh My! Such a blessing. The preaching and the 'sanging'. Felt like I'd been to a revival."

"Well, Mrs. Glenn we are having a contest and wanted to ask you one question. If you answer correctly, we have a very special gift for you."

"Can you give me time to stir my peas? I'll be right back," she said.

"Yes, ma'am."

Robert and I had all of thirty seconds to belly laugh and Lois was back.

"I'm back. Just didn't want to burn my peas."

"No ma'am. Are you ready for your question?"

"As ready as I'll ever be. What is it?"

"Mrs. Glenn, can you quote John 3:16?"

"Why yes, I believe I can:

For God so loved the world that He gave His only Begotten son that whosoever believeth in Him should not perish but have everlasting life."

"You are right," Robert said with a 'Bob Barker style' voice. I am happy to tell you that you have won an all-expense paid trip to North Carolina. You will be spending the weekend with Billy and Ruth Graham."

"Oh my! You don't mean it!!"

Robert and I were coming apart. He had maintained his composure for as long as he could. I took the telephone receiver.

" Mrs. Glenn, this is Ann here at WELO. I need to get your information please ma'am."

"Oh honey, I'm just beside myself. Can you call back after dinner?"

"Why yes ma'am, I'll be happy to. Talk to you a little later." Click.

Robert and I were rolling in the floor. Then we were jumping around like hyenas. Of all our tricks, this was the best yet. Robert didn't know Lois like I did, but I could just hear her when Curtis walked thru that door at dinner time.

What she actually did, we had not planned on happening. She immediately called Farmers and Merchants Bank where her daughter Shirley worked. The switchboard operator said, "Shirley, your mama is on line one and I believe she's crying."

Shirley grabbed the phone, "Mama, what's wrong?"

There was a brief silence and Lois simply asked "Do you have a suitcase?"

"Yeah, an old one. Why? Where are you going?"

"To visit Billy and Ruth Graham in North Carolina."

"Mama, do you feel ok. I'll be right there to check on you. I'm afraid you are having a stroke."

"No, I'm not. Bring that suitcase."

Shirley, knowing she would have to drive from Baldwyn (6 miles), calls Mama and says, "Trixie, I'm afraid Mama is having a stroke. Can you go stay with her til I can get there and get Daddy out of the field?"

Mama walked as fast as she could, less than a half mile to get to Lois. Lois was going through her clothes when Mama walked in.

"Lois are you ok?"

"Oh Trixie, you are never going to believe this, I'm going to Billy and Ruth Graham's for the weekend."

"Have you taken your blood pressure medicine?" Mama asked.

"Of course." Lois said as she waved her hand to dismiss the question. "Let's go sit on the porch and I'll tell you all about it. Shirley is bringing a suitcase, so I can't pack right now anyhow."

Mama sat in the swing and Lois in a side chair.

"Go ahead and tell me what makes you think you're going to visit Billy and Ruth Graham."

"Well, I had my peas and okra on and had cooked a few taters and fried Curt and me two pieces of chicken each, one for dinner and one for supper. I sat down there at the kitchen table and peeled a few apples and put a cobbler in the oven. About that time the phone rang. It's a thousand wonders I didn't burn that cobbler, but after I hung up with the radio station folks I got it out in the nick of time before I called Shirley."

"You talked to somebody at the radio station?"

"Yeah, a man mostly and a woman at the end. They called me and wanted to know if I 'seen' any of the Crusade last week. I told them that me and Curt came to y'alls house three nights and enjoyed every minute."

Then, with her apron up in her hands she began to cry, "Trixie," she sobbed, "of all people, I'm going to see Billy and Ruth Graham. I don't have clothes like they wear, but I've got that new black polka dot dress Curtis bought me in the 'sprang'. Do you think that'll be ok?"

"Lois, what did the folks say to you?"

"Well, the man said if I could answer a question I'd win a prize. He asked me to quote John 3:16 and I did. Then he told me the prize." Tears began to flow again.

Shirley arrived, and Mama told her she'd be right back. Shirley said, "Trixie, it's too hot to walk. Take my car. Mama never had a driver's license but drove around in the community. She came to Ma's and Pa's house. Mama was a good detective or maybe she just knew her daughter.

Keylon and Patricia were outside playing. "Where's Linda Joy and Robert Edd?" she asked. When Mama used double names, it meant trouble!

She marched in the living room and even though she was only 5'1", she looked like a giant.

"What are y'all trying to do? Give a 'body' a heart attack?"

In unison, "no ma'am."

"I know y'all played a trick on Lois and she's out there packing to go to see Billy and Ruth Graham." I wanted to laugh so badly but I knew better.

"Y'all get in that car and I'm taking y'all to apologize. Do y'all hear me?"

"Yes ma'am!"

"And young lady, if you so much as touch that telephone, I'm gonna wear you out. Do you understand me?"

"Yes ma'am."

Shirley went back to the bank after she ate her lunch. Curtis returned to the field. Lois had a tub full of butterbeans she had picked right at 'day light'.

Mama said, "After dinner, me and Linda Joy will come back and help you shell 'em butterbeans. You'll be into the night shelling by yourself."

We ate, walked back to their house and shelled butterbeans until almost supper time.

That morning was a lot more fun than the afternoon.

My Bundle of Early Life

Daddy and the Greased Pig

Daddy lived through the depression and never forgot it. He was an excellent money manager; he just never had a lot to manage.

The first years of my parents' marriage were a real struggle, but I look back at their tenacity and willingness to work hard and I am so grateful for the lessons learned. Can only wish I had learned more.

I remember Ma Gholston and Mama telling me about Daddy's determination that we have pork in the winter of 1948. In early September he heard that a "greased pig" contest would be held at the Fair and Livestock Show in Tupelo. He kept telling the family that he could catch and hold on to the pig. Pa Gholston jokingly said, "Son, you catch it and bring it home, I'll buy the feed to finish it out." 'Finish it out' meant getting it to the size to have a 'hog killing.'

On the night of the "greased pig" contest, Mama dressed me, and we went to the fair with Curtis, Lois and Shirley Glenn. Shirley was twelve, so she probably enjoyed some rides. At eight o'clock, which was normally bed time for Mama, Daddy and me, they announced the "greased pig" contest and asked everybody who wanted to try to catch the pig to come forward. Daddy and a host of other guys lined up. Mama said twelve were let in the pen and were told they had three minutes.

Mama, Lois, and Curtis looked but Daddy wasn't in the pen. A young shoat (young male hog) that was very greasy was let into the ring. All twelve went after him with no luck. Mama said it was so funny to watch. Guys running over each other, one occasionally getting his hands on the pig only to have it slip right through his fingers. At the end of three minutes no one had captured the pig.

All twelve of the grimy, filthy guys crawled out of the pen. The hog was given fresh water and feed. Fifteen minutes later the second group, the last group entered the ring. This time they saw Daddy. He had on overalls. Mama said the bell sounded and eleven of those men scrambled in after the pig. They missed. Daddy was just walking around the pen watching them as they got to their feet, tried to clean up some, and dove in again. Same results.

As they were wallowing around in the pig pen Daddy went in pursuit of that pig with great speed. The pig zigged and zagged and so did Daddy. Mama said everyone gathered around them could hear Daddy saying, "Piggy, piggy, piggy."

Finally, with thirty seconds left on the clock Daddy caught the pig near his rear. The hog was greased so it slipped right out of Daddy's hands. Daddy sprang to his feet, pursued the pig and caught him around his neck and Mama said they flipped and flopped on the ground several times but Daddy held on. He stood to his feet holding the pig just as the three-minute buzzer rang. Daddy won the pig!

Daddy was covered in mud and pig poop, so he rode in the back of Curtis' pickup truck with the pig. When we got home and put the pig in a stall at the barn.

Early the next morning, Daddy showed his pig to the family. They fed his prize pig corn and Pa was true to his word and bought hog feed.

In January they had a hog killing. It dressed over three hundred pounds Daddy told me. He said, "Linda Joy, you loved the ham, sausage and bacon I provided us by catching a greased pig."

Who wouldn't love the ham, sausage and bacon?

Linda Gholston

Honey Bee in Diaper Shirt

July 1957 found Keylon nine months old. He could crawl like crazy and was beginning to say a few words or more accurately, make a few sounds such as Mamma, Dada and Bye. Then he started crawling to the coffee table and pulling up to a standing position. Mama immediately put his hard-soled Buster Brown shoes on him, so his arches wouldn't fall. (Folks believed if babies stood barefoot they would live with fallen arches.)

Oh! I was so excited! My baby brother was about to walk. This became my mission in life – to teach Keylon to walk. So, every day I would practice with him only to have him sit flat on the floor the minute I turned loose of his hands.

Mama kept saying, "He'll walk when he gets ready". But I was ready. After three weeks of committing a lot of time to teaching that child to walk, he just wasn't getting it. I knew he could. I just had to figure out how to inspire him.

One day Mama folded a quilt and put it outside. She sat Keylon in the middle and said to me, "I'm going to wax the living room floor. You watch the baby. When he crawls off the quilt, just put him back."

"Yes, ma'am."

"Don't let him put grass in his mouth."

"No, ma'am I won't."

"Get ya'll some toys cause I don't want you walking on the floor for at least two hours."

So, I went in and got him some toys and a little plastic tea set I had gotten at Christmas. We played for a while and then I thought 'this is the perfect time for him to walk and Mama will be so proud of me'. How was I going to do it? What would make Keylon walk?

As I was pondering this I heard something buzzing. I looked over at a bush just under the bedroom window and there must have been a hundred honey bees flying around. My first impulse was to run. Then, it was like a light bulb!! Of course! If a honey bee would cause me to run, surely it would make Keylon walk. What a great idea! Mama was going to be so proud of me when she looked out and saw her son walking in the front yard!

I jumped up from the quilt pallet and got one of the pink plastic tea cups and a saucer to use as my lid. I gently moved over to the bush where the bees were enjoying nectar. Really afraid of them, I had a hard time getting close enough to capture one in my tea cup. I looked back and there sat Keylon. I could, so clearly in my mind, see him walking like a little prince, so my courage finally matched my stupidity, and I captured a tiny honey bee.

Totally confident I was doing a brilliant thing, I held the saucer over the cup and pulled Keylon's diaper shirt open at the neck and poured the content of my cup into his shirt. Instantly he began to flail his arms and scream 'bloody murder'.

"Walk! Walk!" I insisted.

Mama flung the front door open and dashed into the yard "What on earth is wrong with him?"

"Don't touch him, Mama, he's about to walk."

"Girl, I've told you a hundred times he's not ready to walk. What have you done?"

I told her as she gathered him up. It only stung once, and I was sorry she grabbed him before he walked.

"Go get me a switch! Now!"

"But Mama - - -."

"Don't 'But Mama' me. Get the switch and bring it inside."

I got a switch and walked in. She was putting ice water on Keylon's back. He was already smiling and reached out for me to take him. I did. Mama looked at Keylon, shook her head and said, "Son, she just put a bee on you and now you want her to hold you. Maybe your judgment will improve with age." It has.

Over the years Keylon and I have laughed about the honey bee incident. Thank goodness he has a forgiving heart!

That day began for me a learning curve. Teach, inspire, motivate but most important be patient. Children mature according to their God given nature. Nurture them, believe in them and practice with them. In their time, they will master "walking."

Oh! I also have learned that a "honey bee in the diaper shirt" never works with children or adults!

Young Joe B

Roads surely change in a lifetime. When I was a kid we lived on 'Pratt Road' with a wooden bridge just west of our place. The road was gravel with deep ruts during the cold, wet winter. Only a few cars or trucks would be seen on most days. Today, that road is a state highway with constant traffic.

Pa Gholston knew every vehicle that passed by our farm, and he would often engage in conversation (with himself) about who was going where. Today many vehicles are passing this way but once. They are simply following a GPS to get from point A to point B. The wooden bridge is now concrete, and we never have to worry about ruts so deep that mufflers can be pulled from cars. Those were the days!

December 1959 was very cold with lots of rain. Traffic was light especially after dark. One night when Keylon was three, he was perched on the arm of a huge white chair that sat in our living room near the big picture window; I was sitting in the chair reading a story to him.

Before I could look up from the book, he shouted, "Look Ninna, Look!" I saw what had his attention. A car was slowly turning off the muddy road into our drive. We watched to see if it was someone simply turning around or actually pulling into our drive.

In a second it was obvious the car was pulling into our yard. Daddy was adding wood to the fire and Mama was in the kitchen. Both came immediately to look out of the picture window with Keylon and me.

Daddy said, "That looks like LeRoy's car."

Mama glanced at the clock and added, "It is his car. It's after seven. Surely they are not coming for supper. Out of luck here."

The motor shut off as did the lights. Daddy turned the front porch light on and we saw Uncle LeRoy, Aunt Susie and Becky begin to open doors and step out trying to miss mud puddles.

Soon they were inside, shedding coats and getting near the fire to get warm. Mama said, "Have y'all had supper?"

"Yes, we got hamburgers at Lindsey's Café before we left Baldwyn," Aunt Susie said.

Mama and Aunt Susie were twins and enjoyed an uncanny ability to know when something was going on out of the ordinary with the other. Eating hamburgers in Baldwyn at six o'clock was not ordinary but Mama had no premonition about Aunt Susie or anything going on with her.

Keylon jumped into Uncle LeRoy's arms and they began to play. I got up and gave Aunt Susie my chair near the fire. She looked at the flames as she removed her coat and scarf. Then, looking right at Mama she said, "Dr. Gene's office was covered up. A lot of colds and flu."

"Ya hadn't got it, have you?" Mama asked.

"No, no I'm just fine." Aunt Susie answered.

"But you've been to the doctor?" Mama replied.

"Uh huh, I have," she said.

Finally, she laughed and kinda shouted, "I'm pregnant."

Holy Cow! Becky was born in 1946 and now Aunt Susie was having another baby in 1960! This caught everybody by surprise.

On June 17, 1960, Joe Butler Blassingame arrived! He was a healthy bouncing boy. Unlike Keylon, he didn't suffer from respiratory problems. He could not, however, tolerate dairy. Cow's milk made him very sick. Daddy had a beautiful jersey cow and looked so forward to supplying the baby his milk. Not to be. He had to be fed a soy product that was very expensive. Joe B flourished. By the time he was three he ruled the household. He was smart, with a good personality and loved hearing about Big Daddy's pranks as much as I always did.

Joe's greatest loves were his tricycle and church. He rode up and down the driveway many miles a day. He also never missed a service at Friendship Baptist Church. I remember the Sunday Joe stopped church. Never was a favorite subject of Aunt Susie's but the rest of the family got lots of laughs at her expense.

This day they were sitting about one third of the way from the back. Becky was sitting with all us young folks on the right side of the church. Uncle LeRoy, Aunt Susie and Joe B. were on the left side. When we stood to sing a congregational song, Joe crawled under the pew in front of them. Aunt Susie reached but missed. He was gone. He emerged at the front of the small church. He looked back. Aunt Susie motioned for him to come back. He shook his head vigorously. A prayer was offered, and Joe sat on the step leading to the pulpit area and stayed very quiet. As the prayer ended, Aunt Susie started down the aisle to apprehend Joe.

He was faster and got back to the first pew, and under he went. She was now at the front of the church chasing her three-year-old in front of the entire congregation. Joe crawled and squirmed to the last pew. He saw his Mama's shoes as she came down the aisle toward him, so he turned and went back to the front.

Aunt Susie was so embarrassed she slipped back into their pew beside Uncle LeRoy. Perhaps she would have stayed except when Joe B. came out at the front and realized his Mama was not pursuing him, he began to bang on the piano and sing "I'll Fly Away". So down the aisle Aunt Susie went with haste, but he had gotten under the front pew again. The preacher had paused his sermon and everyone on that side of the church was trying to catch

Joe B. Uncle LeRoy finally got a hold on one of Joe B's shoes, and he wasn't letting go. Joe B and his Mama went outside. It was sometime before they returned, and he sat quite as a church mouse for the remainder of the service.

The summer Joe B turned four he went to the morning revival service on Monday with Ma Butler due to Becky having a dental appointment. Ma Butler was always prepared. She wrapped Joe two tea cakes in wax paper and fixed him ice water in a pint jar. With the lid secure she put the water and tea cakes in a small paper bag. He ate one tea cake and drank a little water during the

song service. Ma Butler was intently listening to the preacher and didn't notice that Joe B had taken his water and moved down the pew a few feet. He was very quiet, and she was so enjoying the service.

Joe B., being kin to Big Daddy, decided to play with his pint of ice water. He silently opened the jar and let a few drops hit the pew. He realized the bench slanted slightly toward Ma's end. He dropped a few more drops and they stopped just short of where she sat. He realized Ma was totally absorbed in the sermon, so he poured some cold water onto the pew --- more than he intended. Almost instantly the cold, wet substance hit Ma's rear. She jumped straight up and yelped. Realizing what had happened and being sorely embarrassed, she too took Joe B. outside for a thrashing!

Joe B. grew into a fine man. He dedicated his professional life to education, retiring as Principal of Baldwyn Elementary School. To this day, he continues to be an active member of Friendship Baptist Church. He serves as a deacon, Song Director and Chairman of the Cemetery Committee.

My Bundle of Early Life

Broken Crayons Still Color

It felt so odd walking into the Pratt Schoolhouse in the summer of 1958. School had been out since May and the old building would never be a school again. To me, it seemed to know that its initial reason for existence no longer existed. Even though the weather was hot and humid, the schoolhouse felt cold, stale, lonely, a structure that had lost its purpose.

Aunt B had asked me to go with her to the school. This was the only place she had ever taught and perhaps her sadness bled over to me. Being there gave me the 'creeps' until she gave me a job.

"Linda Joy, take this box and go in all the classrooms and up on the stage. Gather up any pencils you find and crayons. You can soon start teaching Keylon to color."

"Yes ma'am."

I took the box and started searching in my most recent classroom that housed the fifth and sixth grades. I found two used pencils and four pieces of crayons, then on to the third and fourth grade room where I had better luck. I found two more pencils and nine half or more used crayons. Then to the first and second grade classroom where there were no pencils but about twelve or thirteen crayons. All used, some more than others.

Aunt B was sweeping just beyond the stage in the auditorium. She seemed deep in thought, probably reflecting on her career at Pratt and all the students she had taught. B was the type teacher who saw that each student got what he or she needed. When she sensed that someone was coming to school hungry she would take leftover biscuits and sausage. Then, she would put a nickel in the coffee can at dinner time and tell them to get in line.

"B, I found a few pencils and several colors but they're all broke."

"Broken crayons still color" she said not looking up from her sweeping. To me, at ten, I took her statement as literally true, and true it was. I colored a lot and each broken crayon was true to its color.

However, I think B taught me a much deeper meaning of her saying. She was heartbroken that her school was closed but she would go on to the Baldwyn Separate School District and have a stellar career as a teacher and elementary principal until her retirement in 1986.

All of us will be faced with disappointments, setbacks and failures. Fact of life. But, those things that God has put in us as gifts will still be at our core. In other words, "Broke crayons still color."

Linda Gholston

Little Goody Two Shoes

B and I were getting ready to leave the old schoolhouse. In a few weeks B would be a teacher at Baldwyn, and I would be a sixth grader.

"Can I ring the bell one more time, Aunt B?"

"I don't see why not after you help me load these books" as she pointed to ten or so books she had stacked by the front door. "These will go in the trash if we don't take them. You, Robert Edd and Patricia can enjoy them. That one on top I think you can start reading to Keylon in a few months."

I grabbed several of the books and put them on the back seat of her car. I didn't even glance at the titles. I wanted to ring that bell one more time. During school it was a real treat to be chosen to ring the bell each day. Ringing the bell was based on academic achievement and conduct. Needless to say, I had not been chosen often to ring the bell. But, today there was no competition. The cord had not been pulled since school was out in May. This was my opportunity!

B put a few things in her car and walked back to the flag pole. Today there was no flag flapping in the breeze. In fact, there was no breeze. Just hot, stale air as was typical of early August in Mississippi.

"Go ahead and ring it and let's get home and unload these books," B said softly.

I pulled the cord with all my strength, and the bell began to clang. I was loving it!

Aunt B screamed, "Run! Red wasps!"

I looked up to see a swarm of wasps that obviously had built a nest in the old, quiet bell. We both ran to her car, jumped in and slammed the doors.

"You stung?" B asked.

"No ma'am. You?"

"No, thank goodness. It must have been a hundred or more," B said. Then she added, "I guess they can stay there. That bell won't be rung again to begin a school day."

We rode in silence. It was a short trip being that we only lived a couple of miles from the schoolhouse.

B said, "Let's put these books in the bookcase down in the hall." It was a homemade, three shelf bookcase that stood just outside Uncle Bulich's little bedroom. We got them all on the second shelf as I told Ma Gholston about the wasps. She looked me over to make sure I wasn't stung. I wasn't.

Mama and Keylon came in the front door about that time. Soon to be two, Keylon was very verbal.

"Where you been, Ninna?" he asked.

"To the schoolhouse with B."

"You swing me?" He asked with a sheepish grin that usually got him what he wanted.

"Sure thing," I said and out the door we went. As we swang and laughed I soon forgot about books, bells and wasps.

Keylon's second birthday came and went. It was actually closer to his third birthday that B asked me, "Did you ever read Keylon that book we got for him at the old school?"

"No ma'am I didn't," I replied. I wanted to say that I didn't really want to read it to him, but I didn't.

She pulled it from the shelf. It was old and tattered.

I read the title, "The Story of LITTLE GOODY TWO-SHOES."

Thumbing thru it I realized this was a long story.

"Do you think he'll like this?" I asked.

"I think so. The reading will be good for you. Take it home with you and let me know what Keylon thinks."

Why couldn't B read it to him I wondered?

In September 1959, Keylon had a long siege of bronchitis, tonsillitis, and sinusitis. He was pretty sick for about three weeks. Mama called Dr. Gene Caldwell's office after the first couple of days. Polly Parker, Mama's aunt, worked there and said, "Trixie, we are seeing so much sickness Dr. Gene said to come about six o'clock. The waiting room should be empty by then. I'll disinfect best I can."

So, at six we walked into Caldwell Clinic with a very sick boy. He got a shot and screamed his head off. Daddy held him firmly and the injection was over in an instant.

"Keep him in for a week," Dr. Gene said. "We have to prevent pneumonia if possible. I don't like the sounds of his breathing. Give him all the liquids he'll take and call me if he gets worse."

We got in the pick-up and Keylon was still whining. "Do you want me to read you a book when we get home?"

"Uh huh, I do" he said.

We stopped by the grocery store to get Keylon some orange juice and headed home.

Mama got Keylon in pajamas, the kind with feet. He was sick but had not forgotten my promise of reading to him.

"Ninna, read me a good book."

"Well, B got you this one at the old schoolhouse. Do you want me to read it?" I held the front of the book for him to see the pictures.

"Uh huh I do," as he coughed and crawled into my lap.

I read the title to him, "Little Goody Two-Shoes"! He nodded approval and I opened to the first page. Within the first few pages, the little boy and girl lost their father and then their mother. (Probably not the best story for a less than three-year-old but books were not abundant)

I continued to read, and when I got to the place that Little Goody Two Shoes lost one of her shoes Keylon began to sob.

"Sad Ninna sad," he sobbed.

Mama came from the kitchen. I told her what happened.

"Well, he's sick. Just wait until he's well to read that one again."

"Yes ma'am."

About a month later when Keylon felt good he came to me one night wagging that book.

"Read Ninna."

"Will you listen and not cry?"

"Uh huh, I will Ninna."

So, I started at page one and read the sad story once again. At exactly the same place in the story Keylon began to sob. It just broke his heart.

Mama and Daddy told me not to read that book again until he's older. So, Mama took the book to their bedroom. Keylon begged but she always said, "No" so we read nursery rhymes.

About six months passed and Keylon found the book. By now he was about four and loved all books. So, we tried again with the same results.

This time Mama forbade that I ever read "Little Goody Two Shoes" to him again. This time she hid it like Santa with toys at Christmas.

When Keylon was almost five Mama was cleaning the closet and there was "Little Goody Two Shoes"! Keylon was thrilled. He begged me to read it. Mama said, "If I hear any crying I'm going to whip both of you."

"Ninna, I won't cry. I'm a big boy. Please, Ninna, read it."

So, I started at the beginning. We made it through the Daddy dying, the mama dying and the kids being alone searching for food.

Just as Little Goody was about to lose her shoe, Keylon said, "Ninna, we are about to get whipped if you read any more."

I closed the book and held him tight. His big heart just couldn't take it. Thank goodness he had the sense to realize it.

After Keylon started first grade the teacher asked that they bring their favorite book for "reading" time. He took "Little Goody Two Shoes" and for the first time listened to the entire book without crying.

Linda Gholston

In appreciation…

Jan, who encouraged me to write these accounts. One day I was telling a childhood memory and she simply said, "God has blessed you with a vivid recall of your childhood, and it would be a shame if those who call you GAL don't have them recorded." Thank you, Jan, for this and your continued encouragement.

Patricia, who has typed and retyped with diligence and patience. Because of our long work association, she is the only one who can read my writing. Thank you, Tricia.

Brenda (Sam), my artist and high school friend who read and illustrated several of the stories. She has never produced any sketches for others though asked many times. I feel very honored.

Brenda Ragsdale, who illustrated the cover and several stories. She is my neighbor and I never knew she was an illustrator. Now she is my friend.

Nicole, Liberation's Publishing who has put my ramblings in an acceptable arrangement and birthed a book! I shall forever be thankful for meeting her, and immediately recognizing her strong Christian faith!

Nannette, my cousin and friend who spent hours reading and correcting *My Bundle of Early Life*. Improving heartfelt writing is a kin to telling someone "Your baby is ugly." Many, many times she gently said, "Your baby will look better if…"

To Those Who Call Me 'GAL'

Great is thy faithfulness,
O God My Father,
There is no shadow of turning with thee;
Thou changest not, thy compassions, they fail not
As thou has been thou forever wilt be.

Summer and winter and springtime and harvest,
Sun, moon, and stars in their course above
Join with all nature in manifold witness
To thy great faithfulness, mercy, and love.

Pardon for sin and a peace that endureth
Thine own dear presence to cheer and to guide
Strength for today and bright hope for tomorrow
Blessings all mine, with ten thousand beside!

Refrain
Great is thy faithfulness!
Great is thy faithfulness!
Morning by morning new mercies I see;

Linda Gholston

All I have needed thy hand hath provided;

Great is thy faithfulness, Lord unto me!
Thomas O. Chisholm, 1923

To everything there is a season, A time for every purpose under heaven:

Ecclesiastes 3:1

Mama and Daddy at their 50th Wedding Anniversary July, 1995. Dozens of friends came out.

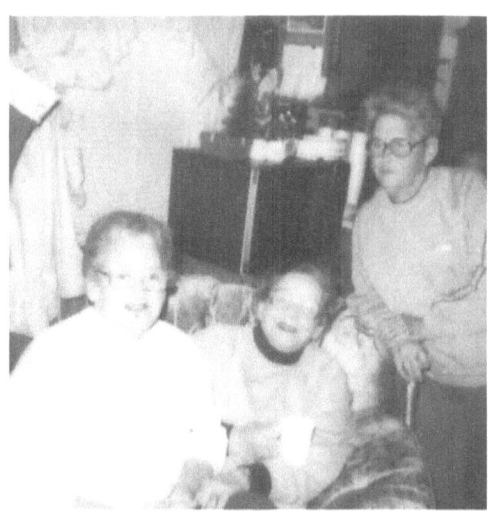

Mama, Aunt Susie, and Aunt Tannis enjoying Christmas in the 1960's

Mama and Aunt Susie as teenagers.

Keylon at 3 ½ years old.

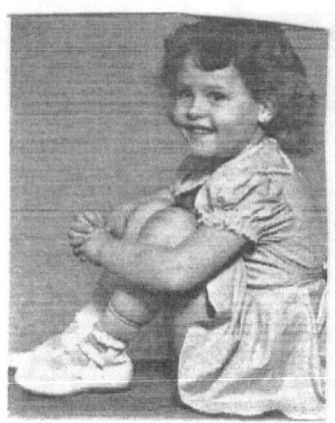

Aunt Tannis took me to Norman's Studio for this picture. I was 2 ½ years old.

Keylon in elementary school at Baldwyn.

Daddy at age eight at Pratt School. Douglas E. Gholston

Above Standing from left: Edwone Gholston, Lorene Gholston, Bulich Gholston, Douglas E. Gholston, Trixie Gholston.

Seated from left: Lula B. Gholston, Robert Edd Gholston, Patricia Alice Gholston, Sophrona Alice Gholston, Marcus D. Lafayette Gholston, and Linda Joy Gholston.

This picture was made at a family reunion in 1953. We were in Itawamba County at Uncle Bonie Gholston's home.

This is Mammie's house where she lived with her son, Arnold Lee Young; her daughter, Brevard Young Bailey; and Mama Brevard's daughter, Belle Bailey.

This is Mammie (Pinkie Herring Young). On her left is Mama Brevard and on her right is Ma Butler (Rosie Young Butler).

Uncle Leroy and Aunt Susie Blassingame with their daughter, Becky. Their picture was made in the late 1950's.

From left: Lula B. Douglas, Bulich, Lorene and Edd Gholston

Uncle Marvin as a student and a soldier. Born Dec. 10th 1922 Died May 22nd 1945

Curtis and Lois Glenn with their only child, Shirley. Lois was the daughter of Mama Brevard Baily. This was made in the 1940's

Big Daddy and Ma Butler. This picture was made in 1978 at Keylon and Teresa's wedding.

This is the house that Ma and Big Daddy built in 1957 after their big house burned. They lived the rest of their lives in this house. Big drew the plans in the dirt after they lost their house and everything they owned.

My Bundle of Early Life

This picture was made shortly after the cow stepped on my foot- "How Many Cows?" Thank goodness my sock clad foot doesn't show!

Mama and Daddy had no money for studio made pictures. Occasionally, Aunt Tannis would say, "Peek-a-boo on Saturday we are going to get your picture made." This picture was made in 1951.

I attended first and second grades in the room on the right, taught by Mrs. Winnie Pratt. My third and fourth grades were in the room on the left and fifth grade was in a room behind this. We had three large class rooms, an auditorium with a stage, two bathrooms, and a lunchroom.

Keylon, Teresa, Brent, Cole, Clay, and Lakin in 1989

Aunt B was principal at Baldwyn Elementary School until her retirement in 1986. She was the epitome educator. She believed in learning, discipline, fun, and love galore for her students.

B surrounded by her nieces and nephews; Robert, Patricia, Keylon, and Linda.

Ma and Pa Gholston with
their four boys in 1925.
The boys from left to right:
Edwone, the oldest,
Born in 1919
Douglas, the youngest,
Born in 1924
Marvin, Born in 1922
Bulich, Born in 1921

Pa Gholston's parents:
Nathaniel Bonapart and Texanna Hoyle
He was born in 1849 and died in 1911
She was born in 1850 and died in 1911

Pa and Ma Gholston
Marcus D. Lafayette Gholston
Sophronia Alice Philpot Gholston
Pa was born 1880 and died in 1969
Ma was born in 1887 and died in 1964.

The home in Pratt Community where they lived their entire married lives. Here they raised their children and grandchildren..

Linda Gholston

www.ingramcontent.com/pod-product-compliance
Lightning Source LLC
Chambersburg PA
CBHW020355080526
44584CB00014B/1033